BUSINESS SYSTEMS AND INFORMATION TECHNOLOGY

Ron Anderson

PARADIGM

Paradigm Publishing
Avenue House
131 Holland Park Avenue
London W11

© Ron Anderson, 1988

First published 1988

British Library Cataloguing in Publication Data
Anderson, Ron
   Business systems and information technology.
   1. Business firms. Applications of computer systems
   I. Title
   658'.05

ISBN 0-948825-96-0

All rights reserved. No part of this publication may be reproduced, stored in a retrieval system, or transmitted in any form or by any means, electronic, mechanical, photocopying, recording and/or otherwise, without the prior written permission of the publishers. This book may not be lent, resold, hired out or otherwise disposed of by way of trade in any form of binding or cover other than in which it is published, without the prior consent of the publishers. This book is sold subject to the Standard Conditions of Sale of Net Books and may not be resold in the UK below the net price.

Set in Times and Futura by Anneset
Weston-super-Mare, Avon

Printed in Great Britain by Hollen Street Press Ltd,
Slough, Berks

CONTENTS

Preface   v

PART 1   Information technology and business systems   1

1   Concepts of information technology   3
Introduction to information technology; Evolution of information technology; Modern informative technology; Need for technological change; IT and its effect on activities of personnel; Advantages of IT

2   Business systems and the business environment   11
General nature of business systems; Business environment

PART 2   Information and information systems   19

3   Nature of information   21
Information in everyday life; Business information; Information attributes

4   Information systems   28
Nature of information systems; Structure of information systems; Storage of information; Information processing

PART 3   Electronic computers   39

5   Electronic computers: nature and purpose   41
Elements of a computer system; Hardware; Software: operating system; Computer programs; Purpose of a computer

6   Selecting a suitable computer   50
Feasibility study; Volume of transactions; Relative costs of hardware and software; Methods of selection; Tender for contract; Proposals; Cost elements of a computer system; Summary of computer attributes and benefits

PART 4   The mechanics of information processing   61

7   File order and access methods   63
Serial processing of a random order file; Serial processing of a sequential order file; Direct access; Full index; Partial indexing; Self-indexing; Algorithmic address generation; Inverted files

8   File processing   70
Sorting files; File updating

9   Information processing techniques   84
Developing screen displays; Developing dialogue for interactive processing; Menu selection; Command selection keys; Natural language processing; Fourth generation languages; Interactive program; Icons, pointers, drop-down menus and windows

10   Development of information systems   93
Structured analysis and design; Summary of the stages of the structured approach; Automated approach to systems development; Computer-Aided Systems Engineering CASE; Structured English; Flowcharting information systems; Prototyping

PART 5 Computer applications – 1 117

11 Computer hardware and processing techniques 119
Selection of processing method; Batch processing characteristics

12 Processing techniques: on-line processing 126
Purpose of on-line processing; Random enquiry and file updating systems; Microcomputer applications; Multi-user and multi-tasking systems; Real-time systems; Computer hardware for on-line processing; On-line operational considerations; Combined on-line and batch processing

PART 6 Computer Applications – 2 135

13 Menu-based information processing applications 137
Using menu-driven applications; Menu-driven microcomputer-based sales order processing system

14 Menu-driven inventory control system 145
Stock control of raw materials and component parts; Integration of inventory control; Processing operations in inventory control; Output from the inventory control system; End of day routine

PART 7: Computer applications – 3 153

15 Spreadsheets: concepts and practice 155
Spreadsheet definition; Operational features

16 Database concepts 165
Definition of a database; Functional files; Public databases; Types of database structure; Schemas and sub-schemas; Data and device independence; Data dictionary; Database Management System; Fourth-generation language (4GL)

17 Database practice 177
dBASE II – Demonstration 1: Creating and processing asset records; Command file; Demonstration – 2: Creating and processing personnel records; Command file

18 Introduction to knowledge-based systems 200
Characteristics of knowledge based systems; Structure of a KBS; Rules; Dealing with uncertainty; Modus operandi; Development tools; Knowledge based system: processing customers' orders

19 Networks 214
Local area network; Network topology; Bus network; Close-coupled networks; Value-added network; Store and forward networks; Wide area networks

20 What of the future 221
Introduction; Competitive advantage; Fifth generation computers; Communications; Image processing; Desk-top publishing; Operating systems; Artificial intelligence; Program generators; Office support systems; Information centre; Decision support systems

Appendix: Case Studies 229

Index 247

PREFACE

Although there are several books on the subject of information processing and technology, this book attempts to be different: the author has provided a new look at the subject giving a blend of processing methods related to typical business systems and applications. The book is structured in seven distinct parts, each part dealing with an important aspect of the subject. It is logically structured, so that its contents may be studied progressively towards an all-round appreciation of the subject; alternatively, topics may be studied individually on a modular basis, depending upon the needs of the reader.

The general features of information processing and the nature of information systems are dealt with, including the design of screen-based menus and forms and the development of dialogue for interactive processing. Also included is an outline of the use of natural language processing systems and fourth generation (4GL) query languages.

The book is intended as an effective study guide, and also as a firm foundation for obtaining practical hands-on experience. It is hoped these objectives have been met by the provision of numerous practical examples and demonstrations relating to the use of spreadsheets and databases. These may be used in conjunction with relevant software manuals during practical sessions.

Demonstrations of menu-based order processing and inventory control systems are included as a guide to the general characteristics and features of menu-based business systems. Details are also included in respect of batch, on-line and real-time systems, together with a discussion of their hardware requirements.

Factors relating to the selection of a suitable computer are included, as well as guidance on the design and structuring of information systems. The book also contains an introduction to the application of Structured English for specifying the logical aspects of information systems, and an introduction to knowledge-based systems for the purpose of introducing the reader to the branch of information processing referred to as artificial intelligence.

The book should prove invaluable to students studying the subject of information processing, information technology and information systems; these students will include undergraduate students of business studies and information technology and students of the BTEC Business and Finance, Public Administration, Computing and Information Systems, and Distributive, Hotel, Catering and Leisure Services Board examinations. Students of Professional Institute Examinations such as the Institute of Administrative Management and the Institute of Management Services will also find the book useful.

In particular the book will be valuable as a medium for encouraging business studies students of BTEC to integrate their studies. The book provides a background and examples relating to accounting, marketing, stock control and personnel functions.

R. G. Anderson

ACKNOWLEDGMENTS

Mr K. M. Gough for his assistance in the preparation of solutions to sorting problems in Structured English.
BOS Software Limited for permission to reproduce details of their menu-based systems.
D. M. England & Partners Ltd for permission to reproduce details of their relational database.

Part 1
Information Technology and Business Systems

CHAPTER 1
Concepts of Information Technology

LEARNING OBJECTIVES

The objectives of this chapter are to provide an appreciation of the nature of information technology and how it has evolved in business through time. This will provide a basis for understanding the nature and purpose of modern information technology and why it is necessary for businesses to implement technological change to attain a competitive advantage. Further objectives are to provide an understanding of the ways in which the tasks in an organisation are affected by the inception of IT and the benefits to be derived by its application in the various business functions.

INTRODUCTION TO INFORMATION TECHNOLOGY

Information technology may be defined as the acquisition, processing, storage and dissemination of information by means of computers and telecommunications. This information can be vocal, pictorial, textual and numerical. In offices information technology usually means the use of computers to obtain the benefits of high speed and accurate processing of information for administrative and control purposes. Computers are often grouped into local or wide area networks for communicating among themselves; this lets data be transmitted from one factory or office to another during the course of routine business activities. Electronic technology does not merely relate to the use of computers however. It embraces a variety of processes and techniques in an all-embracing converging technology, which includes computing, databases, word processing, spreadsheets, telecommunications and electronic mail.

EVOLUTION OF INFORMATION TECHNOLOGY

Computers record data relating to business transactions as discrete numbers (or *digits*); this allows accounting and other data to be pro-

4 BUSINESS SYSTEMS AND INFORMATION TECHNOLOGY

cessed with a great degree of accuracy. Each number is converted to binary code for internal processing by the electronic circuits. In the past, digital processing was performed by human fingers (also called digits). A more sophisticated method of counting used a counting frame, known as an abacus, which computed the value of items by moving beads along wires on a frame; the position of the beads denoted their value. Computers record data by magnetised spots in the internal memory, which replace the beads and wires of the abacus. The position of each magnetised spot, known as a *bit* (*see* Chapter 5), represents the value of a numeric digit.

In the past several decades, the recording and processing of business transactions has undergone revolutionary changes. In larger businesses the processing of data became mechanised; electro-mechanical accounting or bookkeeping machines were used, which revolutionised the posting of business transactions to ledger cards and related documents. Data which was keyed in could now be printed instead of being written by hand. This speeded up the recording process and enabled several documents to be prepared simultaneously, for instance payroll, payslip and tax and earnings record. The introduction of this technology increased the efficiency of staff due to their higher rate of output.

Electrical calculating machines, known as comptometers, were used for high-speed calculations. These were very efficient when used by a trained operator but slow compared to the speed of modern electronic computers and calculators. Calculations were also performed by crank-driven calculating machines and adding/listing machines.

Addressing machines assisted the handling of mail: the addresses were embossed on metal plates (a form of data storage) and fed into the machine automatically from a feed hopper. Word processing systems have since improved this type of operation with mailmerge facilities for adding addresses to circular documents. Postal franking machines were used (indeed they still are) to speed up mail handling by replacing the process of sticking stamps to envelopes and parcels by franking them automatically.

The era of mechanisation then saw the introduction of punched card data processing equipment which superseded the mechanical accounting machines. This mechanised equipment increased the speed, versatility and flexibility of the accounting routines. The use of such machines enabled data to be *captured* (stored) on punched cards which were then processed by various machines: sorters were used for sorting data and collators for merging master files and transaction files in the form of packs of cards; multiplying punches were used for performing calculations; tabulators with arithmetic and printing facilities were used for adding and subtracting data and printing documents such as payrolls and invoices. The machines were 'programmed' by external wires located in holes in plug boards. The location of the wires in the plug boards specified the data fields to be used in the processing operations. This technology heralded what was to be known as automatic data processing or ADP.

The first generation of computers were extremely large, often filling a room with the various cabinets and devices making up the system. These included the processor, control unit, memory unit, device controllers (for controlling the function of tape decks and disc drives) and printers. The construction of these computers was based on thermionic valves which were to some extent unreliable because they generated excessive heat which caused them to fail regularly. Instructing the computer was very complex and required highly specialised staff both for writing computer programs and for its operation. Transaction data and programs were stored in an internal magnetic memory which allowed direct, speedy access to both data and the processing instructions.

The power of computers is forever increasing but their size is generally diminishing with advances in technology. A notable example of this is the introduction of microcomputers based on silicon chip technology where thousands of transistors and diodes are etched on a single silicon chip no more than 5mm square.

MODERN INFORMATION TECHNOLOGY

All types and sizes of computer are used for the processing and storage of information. They are used not only for routine administrative activities but also for preparing and running business simulation models. Simulation models assess the behaviour of systems when subjected to various adjustments without making physical changes to the structure of the systems. Information technology also includes the use of interactive 'Viewdata' database systems, such as British Telecom's Prestel, where a user can view information provided by someone else. The primary purpose of the technology is to increase the productivity, profitability and cost effectiveness of business operations. This technology is always changing and it is imperative for a business to be aware of the tactics competitors are applying in their quest for efficiency.

A typical feature of the new technology is the provision of what are known as work stations to office staff. Work stations have multi-purpose facilities for performing a range of activities. These activities include: computing; electronic filing and retrieval of documents; electronic mail; databases and spreadsheets; word processing and communication facilities by means of local and wide area networks. The technology reduces the time for preparing and disseminating information to the various parts of an organisation. This is often achieved by providing each location with computing power so that each location can process information. This is known as distributed processing.

NEED FOR TECHNOLOGICAL CHANGE

The business world is highly dynamic, forever changing. At the same time new technological innovations and techniques are perpetually emerging. This dynamic situation requires a business to implement 'change'. It needs to implement new ways of doing old things, or new ways of doing new things. When a business changes in response to technical innovations it can become better able to process the information it needs. This may result in fewer staff being employed, with consequent savings, or in faster processing of the information resulting in more timely decisions. The technology to be harnessed to specific business activities is dependent upon a number of factors such as the increasing or decreasing volume of transactions to be processed and other changing requirements. The use of such new technology, particularly the use of sophisticated electronic machines and equipment, can create problems with employees, including the need to retrain staff and transfer displaced personnel to other sections of the business.

IT AND ITS EFFECT ON ACTIVITIES OF PERSONNEL

Information technology is likely to affect the nature of tasks performed by most employees in businesses of all types and sizes. Business administrators, office managers and accountants tend to use personal microcomputers for planning and problem solving. This may include calculations for the preparation of income and expenditure analysis; break-even calculations; cash flow analysis and financial ratios. They may also use the computer for building and running business models and for preparing sales forecasts and projected profit and loss accounts. When computers and computer programs are used to make predictions in this way they are referred to as 'decision support systems'.

CONCEPTS OF INFORMATION TECHNOLOGY 7

Clerical staff traditionally deal with business transactions throughout all the relevant processes including checking of incoming documents, recording their receipt in a register, performing computations, preparing output documents and recording the transactions in the relevant ledger. In all but the smaller business this situation no longer exists as the work has been delegated to a computer. This leaves staff the task of preparing data for input to a computer which then carries out the processes they previously dealt with. Personnel are now free to spend more time on the conceptual and control elements of systems.

The activities referred to as office services are also likely to benefit from information technology. Office services include a variety of tasks including secretarial, typing, reprographic, postal, telex, filing, telephone, facsimile and other communication services. The incidence of technology in this sphere of activity is quite significant as it includes: word processing; communication facilities in the form of electronic mail and digital PABX systems; and electronic filing and data retrieval systems including free text documents.

The term PABX is an abbreviation for Private Automatic Branch Exchange which refers to a type of private telephone exchange. In the older technology telephone exchanges transmitted voice communications as analog signals—waveforms representing the different tonal characteristics of people's voices. Modern technological developments have introduced the digital PABX which translate voice (analog) signals into digital signals—the same type of signals required by electronic computers and terminals. Digital exchanges enable electronic computers, terminals, work stations and local area networks to be linked together for the purpose of digital transmission of data between the various devices as well as for voice communications. Digital PABX provide the nucleus of integrated office systems acting as message switching centres for routing data or text from workstations, etc.

An electronic diary, a useful facility for the busy secretary or business executive, electronically records the time of meetings arranged by one executive on the diary of others. This is accomplished by a program which stores and displays on request events for specific days. The details can be initiated or amended by the keyboard of the work station.

Home-based Electronic Office
An executive can be equipped with electronic facilities for the purpose of performing business activities at home. The equipment

8 BUSINESS SYSTEMS AND INFORMATION TECHNOLOGY

required consists of: a portable computer terminal; a monitor or domestic television set and an acoustic coupler for connecting the terminal to a public telephone line by a domestic telephone connection point. By this means the terminal is connected to a remote mainframe computer supporting a database. The executive is connected to the computer after dialling its number and then keying in a password which gives access to the computer system. Additional passwords may be required to access specific data stored in the database. The computer is programmed to recognise each executive's password and which files he or she has authority to access. The executive's home equipment may also include a printer enabling reports to be printed locally (*see* Fig. 1.1).

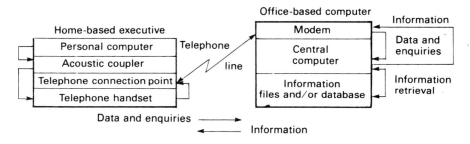

FIG. 1.1 *Home-based electronic office*

ADVANTAGES OF IT

The specific benefits of information technology for a particular business will depend upon a number of factors. It is important to ensure that the technology to be implemented is suitable for the needs of the business; the technology must be cost effective and it must achieve the required level of productivity. It is vital to ensure the right technical solution is applied to a *correctly diagnosed* problem.

Typical benefits	**Manner of achievement**
1 Higher volumes of data processed with fewer personnel	Computerised applications including multi-user and multi-tasking systems
2 Improved information flows	Computerised applications including the use of electronic mail and on-line databases

3	Integration of systems packages	Integrated software
4	Problem solving improved	Decision support systems including the use of spreadsheets and modelling software
5	Improved communications	Local or wide area networks and digital PABX systems
6	More effective accounting	Integrated accounting software
7	Increased effectiveness of branch operational systems	Implementation of on-line systems
8	Speedy storage and retrieval of information	Well structured data files and databases
9	Improved control of operations	Real-time computer systems

SUMMARY OF KEY POINTS

- Information technology relates to the use of electronic technology in the office.
- The purpose of information technology is to increase the productivity, profitability and effectiveness of business operations.
- Information technology assists in the rapid and efficient dissemination of information to all parts of the business.

SELF-TEST QUESTIONS
1. Define the term information technology.
2. In the past several decades the recording and processing of business transactions has undergone evolutionary changes. What are these changes?
3. List a number of features of modern information technology.
4. Why is there a need for technological change?
5. Information technology is likely to affect the nature of tasks performed by business personnel. What form will this take?
6. Electronic technology makes it possible for an executive to work at home. What facilities would be necessary to do this?
7. List the benefits to a business by the inception of information technology.
8. How may the benefits you have listed be achieved?

FURTHER READING

Microprocessors today, Robin Webster, Kaye & Ward, London, 1982.
The electronic office, Malcolm Peltu, Ariel Books, London, 1984.
Electronic life, Michael Crichton, Arrow Books, London, 1984.
The Penguin computing book, Susan Curran and Ray Cusnow, Penguin, London, 1983.
People and chips, Christopher Rowe, Paradigm, London 1986.

CHAPTER 2
Business Systems and the Business Environment

LEARNING OBJECTIVES

The objectives of this chapter include awareness of the nature of business systems, as a basis for understanding their information processing needs. The nature of functional and integrated systems is explained. The different types of systems which exist in most businesses, and the organisation of functions and their need for coordination is described. Further important objectives are an understanding of the business and economic environment in which activities take place.

GENERAL NATURE OF BUSINESS SYSTEMS

Business systems provide organised procedures for conducting business operations. These operations include activities such as payroll processing, financial and management accounting, stock control, personnel administration, marketing and purchasing. The nature and structure of business systems is often dependent upon the type of business and the nature of its activities. A manufacturing business, for instance, requires systems for purchasing raw materials and for planning and controlling production. Banks require a system for controlling investments and loans and insurance companies need systems for processing insurance premium renewals. In the retail industry, shops are supported by point of sale check-out systems and other sales administration procedures. Tour operators and travel agents require systems for dealing with holiday availability and reservations. However all businesses, whatever their nature, require routine systems covering personnel, general office and financial matters (*see* Fig. 2.1).

Functional Systems
Business operations are usually organised according to the nature of the tasks to be performed; this is called functionalisation. A limited

12 BUSINESS SYSTEMS AND INFORMATION TECHNOLOGY

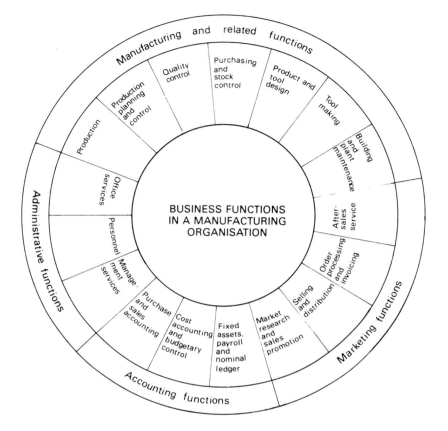

FIG. 2.1 *Diagram of traditional business systems*

range of activities is carried out in accordance with the tasks allocated to each function. In a payroll function, typical tasks include calculating the wages of employees and recording days off due to sickness or holidays. Each function is controlled by a functional manager who is supported by specialists, appointed because of their skill, experience and knowledge in relation to the tasks delegated to them. All businesses are a composition of many small sub-systems, each of which performs a particular activity (*see* Fig. 2.2).

Integrated Systems
Integrated systems are those which combine a number of related activities. Take the example of processing customers' orders. Order details are recorded on despatch notes by the warehouse. The quantity of each item despatched is deducted from the quantity in stock by the stock control system, for stock management requirements. When stock quantities fall below the re-order level (a parameter for ensur-

ing that items are replenished before they finally run out), a purchase requisition is prepared and forwarded to the purchasing department. The purchasing department prepares purchase orders which are sent to the relevant suppliers. A copy of the despatch note is sent to the invoicing section for the preparation of invoices which are sent to customers. A copy of each invoice is sent to the accounting department for recording on the respective customer's account. In integrated systems the output from one part of the system provides the input to another. Well designed integrated systems achieve efficiency because they are more representative of the way events occur in the real world.

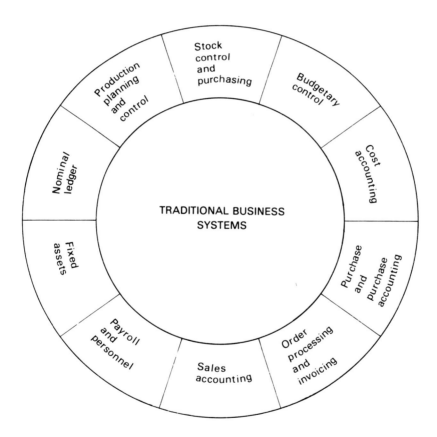

FIG. 2.2 *Diagram of business functions in a manufacturing organisation*

Integrated systems transcend functional boundaries and only need the input of data once. Functional systems often require the input of the same data for different purposes and this creates inefficiency because tasks are duplicated. This situation is overcome by the use of databases consisting of structured non-redundant data. The data needs to be stored only once and can be retrieved by authorised personnel in the various functions.

Financial Systems

Financial Accounting Systems
Systems are required for all financial accounting activities including the recording of transactions in proper books of account. The term 'proper books of account' must not be taken too literally in this modern technological age because they may consist of computer printouts in loose leaf form. It is generally only the smaller business which nowadays records transactions in traditional bound ledgers. The focal point of a financial accounting system is the nominal ledger which records the totals of all types of transactions relating to sales, purchases stocks and other assets—buildings, plant and machinery, cash at bank. From the details in the nominal ledger, accounting information such as balance sheets, trading accounts and profit and loss accounts are prepared. Internal check procedures are another important part of financial accounting systems; these ensure the integrity of accounting data and the detection of fraudulent conversion of records. Systems are also required for controlling the receipt and payment of cheques and petty cash payments and the preparation of monthly statements of account which inform customers of the amount they owe. Statutory records relating to wages and salaries and VAT, etc. must also be prepared by appropriate routines.

Management Accounting Systems
Systems are required which enable managers to manage a business's finance: management accounting activities include the preparation of financial control information usually presented in the form of departmental operating statements. Such statements include: cost and budget data relating to different classes of expenses; variances from planned results; and operating ratios. A typical operating ratio might relate to the level of productivity achieved, i.e. cost effectiveness in the use of resources such as plant capacity or human resources. Variances mean the differences between, for example, budgeted and actual overhead expenses. Budgeting includes the preparation of: cash flow statements; projected profit statements; and balance sheets. These are often prepared by spreadsheets on microcomputers located in the accounting department. In addition systems are needed for evaluating capital expenditure projects.

Non-financial Systems

Production Systems

Systems in a manufacturing business are required for determining standard times for operations; planning and controlling production and computing the output of employees and for controlling the quality of production.

Marketing and Sales Systems

Systems are required for sales forecasting and analysing the data obtained from market research. Credit control is important and systems are needed for performing credit checks on prospective and current customers. Orders must be processed, despatched and stock shortages recorded, despatch notes and invoices must be prepared and sales statistics, including profitability reports, must be produced.

Personnel Systems

Systems are required for administering the human resources of a business including recruitment, administration of pension schemes and procedures for job grading, merit rating and the promotion of personnel.

Purchasing and Stock Control Systems

Systems are required for the procurement of supplies, for all business activities, by placing purchase orders on appropriate suppliers. Follow-up procedures are required for ensuring that orders are received on time, to avoid loss of orders or hold-ups in production due to stock shortages. The purchasing function is sometimes responsible for administering stock control systems in order to avoid a build-up of excessive stocks which incur interest charges if financed by loans or overdrafts. Such systems also avoid stock shortages in order to avoid a loss of profit caused by an inability to fulfil a customer's order. A number of parameters control stock levels, including minimum (safety) stock level, maximum stock level and the level at which stocks should be replenished—the 'reorder level' and the 'reorder quantity'. All stock transactions are recorded on stock records.

Business Functions

Organisation of Functions in the Smaller Business

Small businesses usually group a number of functions together for reasons of economy. For instance personnel administration, payroll processing, correspondence typing, telephone operation, postal services and document reproduction may be combined. These activities would probably be controlled by an administrator with the title of office manager. Another executive in the same company might be responsible for buying activities, planning and control of production and stock control.

Organisation of Functions in the Larger Business
Larger businesses tend to segregate activities on the basis of specialisation rather than grouping them: functions may be separately organised for accounting, manufacturing, personnel, purchasing, production planning and control and stock control. Such specialisation means that each function can be performed more effectively and in large businesses there is enough work involved in each function for specialisation to be efficient and economic.

Co-ordination of Functions
The co-ordination of functions is essential because even though they are separated for administrative convenience they are interrelated, the activities of one affecting those of another. Awareness of this is essential otherwise the achievement of one function will be optimised to the detriment of a related function. This may occur, for instance, when the production function produces large volumes of products to achieve cost effectiveness but overlooks the need of the financial function to minimise the investment in unsold stock sitting in a warehouse.

BUSINESS ENVIRONMENT

Economic Environment
All business activities are conducted in an economic environment consisting of many different types of business. Some businesses serve only the needs of the home market: well-known examples are supermarkets such as Sainsbury and Tesco. Other businesses, such as car manufacturers who produce cars both for home and overseas markets in competition with foreign manufacturers, all vie for an increasing share of the total market. Other businesses operate on an international basis through overseas subsidiary companies possessing both manufacturing and marketing facilities with which to serve the local market. These businesses avoid transportation costs which are incurred if goods are despatched to overseas distributors from home-based factories. Import and export activities are affected by fluctuations in exchange rates which can adversely affect the terms of this sort of trade.

BUSINESS SYSTEMS AND THE BUSINESS ENVIRONMENT

Need for Effective Systems
Economic conditions overseas can change, and exchange rates can fluctuate wildly. This means that powerful computers linked together in a communication network facilitating high speed interchange of information between the various geographically dispersed factories or offices are vital to business operations. World wide communications of this type are provided by telephone cables and satellites making the distance between operational units of no consequence to the effective flow of information in the modern business world.

SUMMARY OF KEY POINTS

- Business systems provided organised procedures and methods for conducting business operations.
- The nature and structure of business systems is dependent upon the type of business and the nature of business activities.
- Business operations are usually structured by function — the nature of the tasks to be performed.
- Integrated systems consist of a combination of related activities.
- Financial systems include financial and management accounting systems.
- Non-financial systems include production, marketing and sales, personnel, purchasing and stock control, etc.
- Business functions must be coordinated.
- Business activities are conducted in an economic environment.

SELF-TEST QUESTIONS

1. What systems are required by a manufacturing business?
2. What is the meaning of the term functionalisation?
3. Give an example of a typical integrated system.
4. What is the underlying reasoning of systems integration?
5. What is the primary benefit derived from integrating systems.
6. What tasks are performed by a financial accounting system?
7. How does management accounting differ from financial accounting?
8. Outline the tasks performed by production and marketing systems.
9. Why is it necessary to coordinate business functions?

FURTHER READING

Management planning and control, R. G. Anderson, Macdonald and Evans/Pitman, London, 1981.
Business Systems, R. G. Anderson, Macdonald and Evans/Pitman, London, 1986.
Understanding organizations, Charles B. Handy, Penguin, London, 1986.

Part 2
Information and Information Systems

CHAPTER 3
Nature of Information

LEARNING OBJECTIVES

This chapter provides understanding of the nature of different types of information and how everyday information both compares and differs from business information. The objectives also include the need to be aware of the important attributes of information which must always be considered in information processing systems.

INFORMATION IN EVERYDAY LIFE

Information can be described as facts relating to situations or topics which impart knowledge or intelligence, and which inform us of matters of interest to us. In normal daily life facts are obtained from observing events and activities; from reading books or magazines; from radio or television; and from information obtained during the course of discussion. As well as these traditional sources of information, there are now technological sources of information such as databases, computer files and knowledge-based systems (*see* Fig. 3.1a). The facts, or data, on their own do not necessarily provide information. To mean anything they must be combined with other facts or presented in a particular way (Fig. 3.1b): data must be processed.

An important but invisible type of information which governs our lives to a greater or lesser extent is information about time. Time dictates when we get out of bed in the morning, when we go to work or college, when we go home, go out and go to bed. In industry, manufacturing operations are measured to assess the time they should ideally take. Computer operations are assessed to establish the time taken by individual computer runs to process data. Information about time is useful for controlling the efficiency of operators, for planning how long different quantities of various products should take to make, and for planning work schedules. In fact, time is an essential aspect of life and one of the first things a computer will display when it is switched on is the time.

Information from electronic sources is becoming more and more

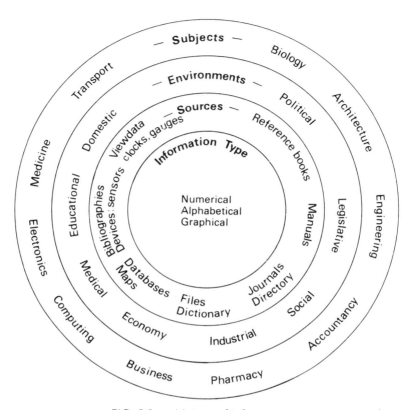

FIG. 3.1a *Nature of information*

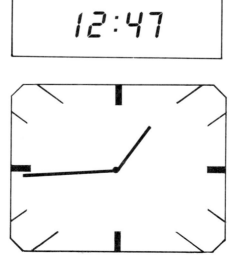

FIG. 3.1b *Similar information can be presented in various ways*

important in everyday life especially in the field of personal banking. Information about your bank balance is always useful. A bank can provide this information to a customer very quickly by keying in a customer's account number on a keyboard connected to a remote computer. The account details are then displayed on a screen. This is an example of an on-line enquiry system which provides answers to random enquiries at high speed. Some banking systems allow customers to do this from their homes, via personal computers connected to the telephone system. Other banking systems allow an account to be debited directly at the 'point of sale' in a shop or at a cash-dispenser; in these cases the information is going from the customer to the bank.

Information about holidays can be obtained either by telephoning or visiting the local travel agent or by consulting a package holiday brochure. The required details are often obtained by the agent keying in the holiday reference on a terminal connected by telephone line to the tour operator's computer. The computer searches its files for the required information. Generally this sort of information transfer is very rapid. However, there can be occasions when on line enquiry systems are slowed down by a large number of enquiries simultaneously—this is known as *traffic density*.

BUSINESS INFORMATION

For a business to operate effectively it needs timely information relating to its various activities in order to control the results obtained and to ensure they are compatible with management requirements. The nature and frequency of providing information is dependent upon the particular function—whether stock control, purchasing, sales or general accounting.

A sales manager in charge of domestic appliance sales needs to know whether he or she is achieving sales targets for each appliance. Information is therefore required of the quantities of refrigerators and other products sold for the current month (or week). This may be combined with information relating to the volume of sales achieved in the corresponding month of the previous year and the previous month of the current year, for the purpose of establishing trends. Sales for the year to date with a comparison of the previous year's sales is also a useful guide.

As well as information about quantity, information about market share is important. A car manufacturing business is extremely interested in knowing its share of the market and whether the trend is increasing or decreasing. If the trend is downwards it often leads to a decision to provide special bonuses to dealers for the purpose of boosting sales, which may require a reduction in showroom prices (*see* Fig. 3.2).

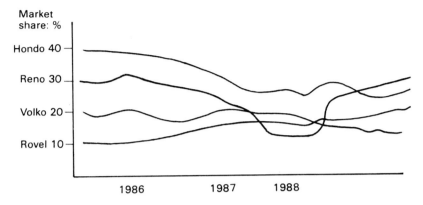

FIG. 3.2 *Car manufactuers: market share trends – graphical information*

A garage proprietor needs to know the number of litres of petrol sold each day for comparison with the amount needed to to be sold to be profitable. The proprietor incurs overhead expenses regardless of how many litres sold, and they must be covered by the profit margin obtained on each litre sold. The proprietor also needs to sell enough petrol to cover the cost of renting the garage premises, payment of rates to the local authority and the cost of insuring and maintaining the buildings and equipment. In addition, telephone, postage and stationery costs are incurred, and the wages of the forecourt attendants (*see* Fig. 3.3).

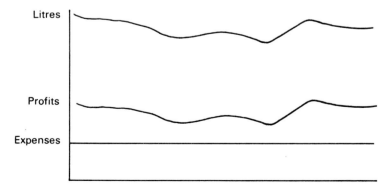

FIG. 3.3 *Garage petrol sales: trend of litres, profits and expenses – graphical information*

NATURE OF INFORMATION 25

A newsagent needs information each day on the number of different newspapers and magazines sold in order to adjust the quantities of each to satisfy customers' demand. He does not want to have too many left over, nor does he want shortages as unsatisfied demand reduces profits.

A factory manager needs to know production targets and information relating to available plant and machine capacity, the quantity of each type of material in stock and the numbers of personnel employed. With this information the manager can match production requirements with availability of resources. The factory also needs to operate economically and to this end information is required relating to production achievements. This means that production volumes can be kept sufficiently high to cover the expenses being incurred in running the factory, many of which are incurred regardless of the level of activity (these expenses are known as *overheads*).

TABLE 3.1 *Summary of types of information*

General information	Business information
Time	Time
Expenses	Expenses
Price of beer	Purchases
Wages	Units sold
Job offers	Sales orders
Oven temperature	Factory temperature
Friends' Addresses	Customer and supplier addresses
Food in the freezer	Utilisation of resources
Cost of the disco	Operating costs
Cost of compact disc player	Cost of machines and equipment
Rail and bus fares	Travelling expenses
How much money in the bank	How much money in the bank

INFORMATION ATTRIBUTES

1 Information must assist managers to make effective decisions, e.g. information relating to the demand for aircraft seats on a specific flight on a particular day is important as it may be necessary to change the aircraft either to a smaller one, a larger one or an additional one depending upon the circumstances. Of course, a scheduled flight would take place regardless of any short term variation in the number of seats booked.

2 It must be suitable for controlling business operations, e.g. business operating costs by means of information produced by a budgetary control system.

3 It must be compatible with its intended purpose, e.g. a system for controlling customer credit necessitates information on the status of customer accounts.
4 Reports should be written in an easily understandable manner to facilitate their interpretation and usefulness.
5 Unnecessary duplication of details (redundancy) should be avoided.
6 Information must relate to current operational circumstances.
7 Information must attain an acceptable level of accuracy. In accounting systems all data must be accurately recorded. Information of a general nature may be acceptable at a 95% accuracy level.
8 It should be capable of being obtained easily and speedily. This is of particular importance in real-time or on-line enquiry systems.
9 It must be produced at an acceptable cost.
10 It should be provided as frequently as circumstances demand. Some information must be provided immediately as events occur for the efficient control of operations, e.g. aircraft seat reservation enquiries.

SUMMARY OF KEY POINTS

- Information may be defined as facts which serve a useful purpose.
- Information relates to facts, situations and events.
- Time is an important item of information.
- Information can be obtained from many sources.
- Information enables decisions to be made.
- Information facilitates the planning of activities.
- Information is valuable for the efficient management of a business.
- Information relates to many different environments.
- Information relates to many different subject areas.

SELF-TEST QUESTIONS
1. What information would a sales manager need to know about sales?
2. What information does a stock controller need to know about raw materials in the stores?
3. What information is required in the wages office of a factory to compute the earnings of employees?
4. What information would you need to compute the value of sales to a customer?

FURTHER READING

Business Information systems, Chris Clare and Peri Loucopoulos, Paradigm, London, 1987.

CHAPTER 4
Information systems

LEARNING OBJECTIVES

This chapter describes the nature of information systems and distinguishes between data and information. It stresses the need to be aware of the importance of management by exception when providing information to management, and the nature of feedback. Objectives also embrace the importance of knowing the structure of information systems, the nature of records and files, and typical information processing operations.

NATURE OF INFORMATION SYSTEMS

Conversion of Data into Information

Data relating to business transactions has to be converted into information for it to help the effective administration and management of a business.

It is important to appreciate that information is produced from data after it has been subjected to a number of processing operations. Data is input to a processing system which produces output known as information. Processing systems in the past were referred to as data processing systems but nowadays they are called information processing systems or simply information systems. Data is a means to an end, not an end in itself; the desired end is the production of useful information, therefore as data processing produces information it is more appropriate to use the expression information systems (*see* Fig. 4.1).

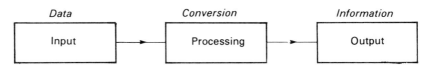

FIG. 4.1 *Stages of information processing*

Management by Exception

Information systems are often enhancements of unsophisticated data processing systems which have been developed to produce information for managerial control and decision making. Information systems normally incorporate the principle of management by exception which restricts reporting to significant facts.

Computerised Information Systems

A computerised system is ideal for supporting an information system because of its ability to respond speedily to enquiries in on-line or real-time systems. (Real-time systems are systems that can allow files to be accessed and updated immediately an event occurs.) The objectives of such systems include the provision of information to all levels of management at the most relevant time, at an acceptable level of accuracy and at an economical cost.

Feedback and homeostasis

An essential element of an information system is its ability to incorporate feedback. *Feedback* is the term used to describe the process of communicating a system's measured output,* from a sensor† to a comparator.‡ The aim is the detection of deviations from budgeted or planned results; these deviations, known as errors or *variances*, are communicated to an effector for the purpose of taking corrective action to attain a stable system (a state of homeostasis) free from unnecessary fluctuations. *Homeostasis* is the process of attaining a stable system, or maintaining a state of equilibrium, to offset the effect of random influences from outside. One example of random influence is the variation in the time which elapses from when an order is placed to when the goods ordered are received, i.e. the lead time. Such variations in lead time can occur due to production and supply problems in the supplier's organisation which can also be caused by random outside influences, like the weather, strikes or illness. Variation in lead time mean that a purchaser's stocks fluctuate which can cause production delays due to 'stock-outs' (shortages). A remedy for this situation is the provision of safety stocks which can be used during the time supplies are delayed. However, while these extra stocks are a useful safety device they do represent an added investment which must be paid for.

---

* A system's measured output defines the magnitude of a system, expressed in terms such as units produced, value of sales achieved or actual cost incurred.
† A sensor may be an electronic device, such as a bar code scanner as used in supermarkets for recording items sold; or it may be a person counting items produced in a factory. It may be a mechanical digital recorder, attached to a machine such as a power press, which counts the number of items processed.
‡ A comparator may be a routine in a computer program for comparing data elements to obtain differences between them; or it may be a credit control clerk checking customers' account balances to assess if they are in excess of the allowed credit limit before accepting an order.

Primary Data

Primary data are facts collected in a number of different ways according to circumstances and the nature of the subject about which information is required. Data of this type may be collected by taking measurements from monitoring devices or sensors which measure the situation at any particular moment: the number of units of gas and electricity consumed to date is recorded on a meter; steam pressure is read from a gauge; the quantity of chemicals, oil or petrol in a storage tank is obtained by means of a dipstick. Primary data also consists of facts and figures of various transactions recorded on primary documents during the normal course of business. Transactions vary greatly among different types of business but typically include bank paying in slips, cash sales notes, stores issue notes and goods received notes. Sometimes primary data is collected in a fully automatic way, such as in supermarkets which have laser scanners to read a commodity bar code; or in banking, where banks have cash dispensing and recording equipment sited externally. Primary data is also used in terminal based operations when files are updated with current events. Primary data on its own is often of little use: but it is capable of conversion into useful information.

Secondary Data

Secondary data is data which is already in existence and which can be retrieved, for instance by consulting business and government statistics or internal records collected for other purposes. Such data may already have been processed to some extent. If this data is used for other than its original intended purpose it is important that it is compatible with current requirements, and that it is complete and up-to-date. It is important to be aware of any inaccuracies in the data as inaccuracies that are not relevant to one function may create ambiguous results when the data is applied for other purposes. Secondary data taken from an internal environment deals with qualitative and quantitative aspects, e.g. performance levels, costs incurred, overheads expended, profits and losses incurred, cash flows, lines of credit, net current assets, quality of management and so on. This type of data is extremely useful for strategic and tactical planning.

STRUCTURE OF INFORMATION SYSTEMS

Records and files store details of specific types of business transaction either for reference or for updating purposes. A business consists of many different elements which are defined as *entities*, examples of which are customers, suppliers, employees, stocks of materials, products and assets. The details describing each entity are known as *attributes*. An example of a product entity with its attributes is shown below. Each attribute consists of fields of information which combined to form a *record*. A record is required for each item classified within a particular entity, for each stock item, each employee, each customer, each supplier and so on.

A *field* is a unit of data; it consists of descriptive or numeric data dependent upon whether, for instance, it is a customer address (descriptive) or the number of units of a specified product sold to a customer (numeric). Fields normally have a fixed number of characters.

The individual records are uniquely identified by a reference number or code combination known as a key which facilitates the sorting, accessing and updating of records. A product entity typically consists of the following attributes or fields:

Entity Type: Product

	Field/attribute
Key field	product code
Alternative key	product description
Other fields	cost price
	selling price
	VAT code
	quantity in stock
	value of stock @ selling price
	value of stock @ cost price
	carriage charges
	re-order quantity
	re-order level

A collection of related records form a file. A file, in effect, is a store of information and typical files to be found in information processing systems include:

    a Stock records–stock file
    b Customer records–customer file
    c Supplier records–supplier file
    d Product records–product file
    e Asset records–plant and machinery file
    f Employee records–payroll, employee or personnel file

32 BUSINESS SYSTEMS AND INFORMATION TECHNOLOGY

The nature of a file is dependent upon the nature and type of business; examples are: details of jobs in process in a garage, to be charged to customers, are contained in a job file; records relating to a bank's customers are stored in a customer file; a hotel may have an accommodation file to provide information on the availability of rooms and a file to record charges incurred by guests; an airline requires a file of available seats on all the different flights and a tour operator requires a file of package holidays available. A file in accounting terms contains accounts and computerised files which are constantly being updated; these are referred to as *master files*. Other files contain details of transactions such as stock movements (issues and receipts, sales, returns). Some files are required for reference purposes and include details such as the name and address of customers and suppliers and details such as hourly rates or piecework rates for wages calculations. These sort of files are updated only occasionally.

STORAGE OF INFORMATION

A clerically oriented system stores records in filing trays or filing cabinets which are accessed manually, whereas files used by computer applications are stored on magnetic media—usually some type of magnetic disc.

The principle of storage is the same but the manner in which they are stored, retrieved, updated and referenced differs. Clerical filing systems contain ledger cards and documents. Each record constituting a file is individually accessible and can be read by personnel as they are recorded in characters that are readable by humans. Computerised magnetic files can only be interpreted by electronic circuitry as the records are recorded magnetically in binary code and stored on segments of disc invisible to the human eye.

INFORMATION PROCESSING

Typical Processing Operations

Processing operations transform data into a useful, meaningful form and typical operations are outlined below. Some of the processing operations are specific to computerised processing but even so many of them are relevant to clerical based systems.

Verifying

Verification is applicable to computerised batch processing applications which requires the conversion of data, initially recorded by hand on source documents, to magnetic coded form on magnetic disc. Part of the coding of the data has to be done by hand and verification is necessary to detect coding errors in order to avoid processing erroneous data. Coding errors occur when the encoding operator depresses the incorrect character key on a keyboard. A different operator, who is verifying the coding by keying in the data gain, is unlikely to interpret the same character incorrectly, or to depress the same key wrongly. The encoder can compare the two inputs and look for differences, which will represent errors. It is important to appreciate that computers cannot recognise handwritten details normally, although special scanners can read printed words (this is known as optical character recognition—OCR). This is why data recorded by hand onto documents must be input into the computer, a process which allows for the possibility of error and creates the need for verification.

Validating
Validation is the process of detecting errors in the initial recording of data, as opposed to encoding the data which is a case for the verification process described above.

Sorting
Sorting of data is a widely used operation for assembling transactions into a defined sequence, perhaps ascending numerical order in a ledger or computer file. Different classes of records will have a specific range of code numbers for reference and identification purposes. Each record in a class will have a unique identification number known as a key field. A sorted transaction file facilitates more effective file processing than an unsorted file.

Calculating
It is often necessary to perform calculations on related variables (values) to obtain numerically quantified data, examples of which include:
  a gross value of goods sold for invoicing purposes = quantity sold × price
  b gross wages for payroll purposes = hours worked × hourly rate

In computerised applications computations are built into a program. The form of the instructions in a program is dependent upon the particular language used to write it. A clerk would perform similar computations either mentally or by using a pocket calculator for entering the value of each variable to obtain the required values.

Comparing

This operation is very widely applied as it serves a useful purpose in many business systems for comparing related items of data. The comparison of variables provides valuable control information, i.e. comparing actual number of litres of petrol sold with the target amount. The difference between the two is of importance to the garage proprietor as it provides a pointer to the garage's profitability. Many control systems are based on the principle of 'management by exception', whereby major differences between planned and actual performance are used as a basis for managerial actions. For instance, budgetary control system compares budgeted expenses with actual expenditure. Significant variances are exceptions to budgeted results and it is only these factors which are reported to the relevant manager. Operational matters which are going according to plan are not reported upon. This enables management to concentrate on important and significant matters which require remedial action. Management by exception is also applied to credit control where the value of credit allowed to a customer is compared with the actual amount owing. A credit in excess of the amount allowed is the basis for action. In a stock control system the quantity in stock is periodically compared with the re-order level and if the quantity in stock is equal to or less than the re-order level a replenishment order is produced to obtain new supplies before existing stocks run out.

Updating

The nature of files was outlined earlier in this chapter. It was seen that records contain details representing the current situation of the real world such as how much is owed by each of our customers, how much we owe each of our suppliers and how many items are in stock. These records are updated with transaction data which, in the case of stock items, includes issues from the stores to production (which reduces the quantity in stock) and receipts from suppliers or returns to store (which increases the quantity in stock). Further details about updating are contained in Chapter 8.

Outputting

The output from computer systems is usually by means of a printer connected to and controlled by the computer. Print-outs normally consist of schedules listing the contents of files and documents such as invoices and payrolls. Exception reports are also printed out which inform management of their operating results, e.g. the level of sales or production achieved, operating statistics and accounting data relating to the utilisation of resources. Output may be presented graphically in the form of charts, histograms or graphs depicting production, stock or sales trends; these can be displayed on a video screen or recorded on a graph plotter. In addition, interactive video systems enable pictures stored on a video disc to be displayed on a video screen for a pictorial representation of information. The output from clerical systems is normally handwritten documents or reports. In some instances documents such as invoices and purchase orders are prepared on a typewriter.

Controlling
Computerised applications generate control totals which are an effective means for controlling the throughput of data. The control totals are compared with pre-calculated batch totals and any difference indicates that transaction(s) have been overlooked or computations performed inaccurately because of a hardware malfunction or faults in the software. Control totals are also employed in clerical systems: prior to processing a batch of documents – a file of invoices to be recorded on the sales ledger for instance – a total is obtained using either an adding/listing machine or a pocket calculator.

Example 1: Wages Computations
A wages clerk receives transaction data in the form of employees' clock cards containing details of the hours each employee has been in attendance at the place of work. The clerk validates the data to ensure it is accurate and conforms to normal values, e.g. the hours worked are not abnormal. Any hours in excess of 40 could be construed as being abnormal unless supported by an overtime authorisation note. The clerk then refers to a file to obtain the hourly rate applicable to each employee. The gross earnings are then calculated for each employee by multiplying the hours worked by the hourly rate. The clerk then extracts data from each employee file, i.e. tax code and National Health insurance contribution rate, other deductions such as savings, tax paid and earnings to date and National Health insurance contributions to date. The current gross wages are added to the earnings to date to the previous week and the tax payable to date is then computed. The difference between the tax payable to date and the tax previously paid is either a refund or deduction for the current week depending upon the level of gross wages earned or whether the employee was absent.

The details so far outlined constitute the input to the system and a number of processing activities which provide the information to be

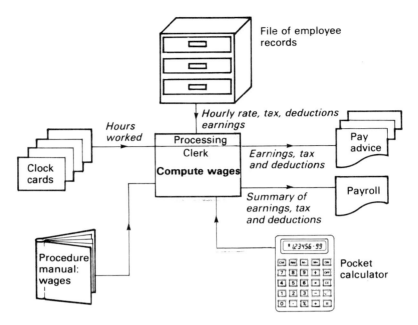

FIG. 4.2 *Clerical wages processing system*

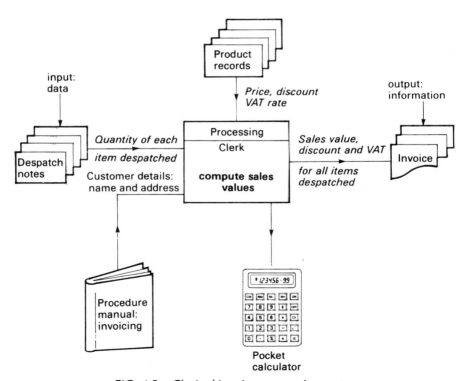

FIG. 4.3 *Clerical invoice processing system*

output from the system. The clerk proceeds to produce the required information by recording the results of the previous computations onto a pay advice slip which informs the employee of his earnings, tax and other deductions for the current week. A summary of all details relating to each employee is recorded on a document known as a payroll which is used for accounting and auditing purposes. The clerk performs all the processing activities from previous experience but has recourse to a procedure manual outlining the processing stages if necessary (*see* Fig. 4.2). The routine for preparing sales invoices is illustrated in Fig. 4.3.

SUMMARY OF KEY POINTS

- Data is the term used to describe details of transactions which are input to an information processing system.
- Information is produced from data after being transformed by processing operations.
- Information systems normally incorporate the principle of management by exception which restricts reporting to significant facts.
- Computerised systems are ideal for supporting information systems as they are able to respond to enquiries speedily.
- Feedback is the communication of a system's measured output to the control system for modifying input to attain a stable state.
- Homeostasis is the process of attaining a stable system offsetting the effect of random influences.
- Primary data consists of transaction details.
- Secondary data relates to facts of a general nature.

SELF-TEST QUESTIONS

1. State the difference between data and information.
2. Why are computerised systems ideal for supporting information systems?
3. Feedback and homeostasis are important features of information systems. Explain why this is.
4. Distinguish between primary and secondary data.

5. What is an entity?
6. What is a field?
7. What is a record?
8. What is a file?
9. List typical processing operations.
10. What is the importance of comparing in information processing?

FURTHER READING

Business information systems, Chris Clare and Peri Loucopoulos, Paradigm, London, 1987.

Data processing 2, Information systems and technology, R. G. Anderson, (6 edn) Macdonald and Evans/Pitman, London, 1987.

Management information systems, Gordon B. Davis and Margrethe H. Olson (2nd edn) McGraw-Hill, 1985.

Part 3
Electronic computers

CHAPTER 5
Electronic computers: nature and purpose

LEARNING OBJECTIVES

The primary objective of this chapter is to provide an understanding of the elements of a computer system and the nature of computer configurations. The necessity of knowing the nature of software is stressed: this includes the characteristics of operating systems, computer programs, instructions, application programs, the role of the computer in business and the wide range of tasks for which a computer is suited and to which it is applied.

ELEMENTS OF A COMPUTER SYSTEM

Digital Computer

The type of computer used for business applications is known as a digital computer because it processes discrete digits, called *bits* of data. The term 'bit' is a contraction of BInary digiT. A binary system is a two-state system consisting of two digits, '0' and '1', where all numbers can be expressed as combinations of 0's and 1's. (For instance 8 is represented as 1000.) The binary system forms the basis of the ASCII code (ASCII is an abbreviation for American Standard Code for Information Interchange adopted as standard by the American National Standards Institute in 1963). This code is widely used on microcomputers and provides the means for transferring data between devices such as from a processor to a printer. ASCII is a 7-bit code which means that characters with binary values from 0000000 to 1111111 can be represented (in other words each character has seven binary digits, or bits). An alternative code is EBCDIC (Extended Binary Coded Decimal Interchange Code) which is used on IBM mainframe computers. The code uses a binary code of 8 bits for each character, or byte (in other words EBCDIC uses an eight bit byte). In this code the letter A is represented by the combination of bits, 11000001. The first four positions are 'zone' bits and the last four are 'numeric' bits. A seven-bit code can provide for

128 different characters whereas an eight-bit code can generate 256 different characters.

Computer Configurations

A computer is not a single machine but a combination of related machines forming a configuration to suit the type of processing to be undertaken, for example, batch or on-line applications. An input device, usually a disc drive or a terminal equipped with a keyboard and monitor screen, transfers data to the internal memory of the processor by data transfer channels and communication lines. The processor may then process the data, i.e. update files by means of the internally stored program and output the updated files to disc storage. Generally there will also be an output device such as a printer for producing documents.

HARDWARE

The processor

The processor, also called the central processing unit or *CPU*, is the main unit of a computer system. It consists of three sub-units:

1 **Arithmetic/logic unit (ALU or AU).** This part of the processor performs arithmetic and logical operations on data. It consists of electronic circuits and registers to which *operands* (units of data to be processed) are transferred and in which results of computations are stored.

2 **Control unit.** The control unit co-ordinates and controls all the hardware comprising the computer system. It acts as a switching device enabling data to flow along the various channels from the internal memory to the AU for processing. Instructions are transferred from the internal memory to the instruction decoder before carrying out instructions. The results of processing are transferred to internal memory locations prior to being output to *peripheral* (i.e. not central) devices such as a printer and disc drive.

3 **Internal memory.** A computer stores data and programs magnetically by two types of internal memory devices. One type is *random access memory* (RAM), which is capable of being directly addressed to obtain access to specific instructions or data; this is an essential requirement for effective information processing. RAM is used for storing application programs and the data to be processed. Instructions can be amended or overwritten and data

replaced as necessary because it is possible to 'write to' and 'read from' RAM. The memory capacity is dependent upon the type and size of computer and varies from 256 kilobytes (256 thousand characters) for personal computers to several megabytes (several million characters) for larger computers. Memory capacity can be increased by adding more RAM chips to the circuit board. It must be appreciated that the contents of this type of memory disappear if the computer is switched off so it is necessary to take precautions by copying files or programs as appropriate to the circumstances.

Read only memory (ROM) is similar to RAM except that it can only be read from not written to. The contents are fixed and cannot be altered. This type of memory is used for storing the operating system as it is important that the operating system is protected from being altered in any circumstances. Personal computers sometimes have a BASIC interpreter stored in ROM which converts program statements into machine code. The contents of this type of internal memory are not destroyed when the power is switched off because its contents have been 'burnt' in during the manufacturing process.

It is important to appreciate that programs are stored on backing storage devices, usually magnetic disc, until required for processing when they are transferred to the internal memory. Instructions can only be executed direct from internal memory and not from backing store (*see* Fig. 5.1).

Processor Characteristics

A *bus* interconnects all the circuitry of a computer system, providing communication channels for input and output transfers to and from the internal memory and peripheral devices. There are various types of bus including a control bus, a data bus, an address bus and a peripheral bus. The address bus connects channels to the internal memory, allowing data to be transferred from their storage locations, using their storage address, to other memory locations for processing. Processors operate at different speeds and have either 8, 16 or 32-bit capabilities. An 8-bit processor only has an address bus of sixteen channels which allows up to 64K bytes capacity ($2^{16} = 65536$). A 16-bit processor may have 20 address channels which provide addressing facilities up to one megabyte ($2^{20} = 1048576$). The results of processing are transferred to an output device such as a printer and/or storage device such as a disc drive (*see* Fig. 5.1).

44 BUSINESS SYSTEMS AND INFORMATION TECHNOLOGY

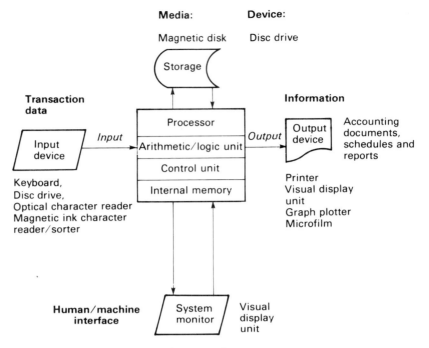

FIG. 5.1 *Elements of a computer system*

SOFTWARE: OPERATING SYSTEM

The operating system automatically performs tasks such as:

- executing and monitoring of input and output operations to ensure data transfers are performed accurately
- checking the status of hardware devices, e.g. a printer, to assess if it is on-line to (connected to) the processor and is available to receive ouput
- attending to the formatting of new discs to be used for storing programs or files
- maintenance of disc directories specifying the programs and files stored on specific discs including the file size or file type
- the amount of unused disc capacity available, i.e. bytes still unused
- disc reading and writing operations
- diagnosing disc errors and executing disc commands such as deletion, copying, renaming and dumping of files
- allocating working area (memory locations) for programs in the internal memory

ELECTRONIC COMPUTERS: NATURE AND PURPOSE 45

- providing for loading programs and chaining between programs
- receiving, interpreting and executing commands input by the operator
- providing facilities for editing commands
- assigning input/output devices to the various input/output ports for data and program transfers
- implementing the use of passwords and providing debugging aids

Three well-known operating systems used on small computers are:

1 CP/M. The operating system CP/M (which is an abbreviation for Control Program for Microcomputers and is the trademark of Digital Research Inc) has a very large software base, i.e. there are many software application packages designed to run with it. There are several versions of CP/M, such as Concurrent CP/M-86, which provides single-user multi-tasking facilities allowing one user to process several programs simultaneously, and MP/M-86, which is a multi-user system for 16-bit computers.

2 MS-DOS. MS-DOS is an abbreviation for MicroSoft Disc Operating System. This operating system has a large software base and, partly because of this, is a popular system. It has been adopted by a number of computer manufacturers, including IBM and Apricot. It is an operating system designed for 16-bit business orientated machines. MSX-DOS is used in the MSX 8-bit machines and Concurrent DOS is used for multi-tasking machines.

3 UNIX. This operating system was initially designed for minicomputers but is now being used on micro computers. It supports multi-tasking as well as multiple terminals connected to a single system. It is widely accepted as the main multi-user system available. Xenix is a multi-user system based on UNIX.

Operating Systems and the Larger Computer
Mainframe computers require very powerful operating systems to control widespread multi-access processing and multi-tasking operations. They provide facilities for high speed switching between users and between programs running concurrently in a multi-tasking environment. Operating systems in this instance consist of the Direct Machine Environment (DME) or Virtual Machine Environment (VME/K) used on the ICL 2950 computer system. Operating systems used by IBM include Multiple Virtual Storage/System Product (MVS/SP) and Virtual Machine/System Product (VM/SP).

COMPUTER PROGRAMS

Instructions

Computerised systems incorporate rules, conditions and actions in a set of instructions known as a *program*. This is the equivalent to a clerk's instructions contained in a procedure manual. Computer programs are stored internally and executed automatically, one instruction at a time. Programs are designed to perform loops to repeat the same sequence of instructions on each transaction. During processing, a program conducts a test to establish the type of transaction to be dealt with and performs a conditional branch to the instructions for dealing with it and then returns to the previous part of the program for dealing with the next transaction or for continuing with the next processing step.

Application Programs

Application programs are special purpose programs for processing specific applications such as stock control, purchase ledger, payroll and nominal ledger, etc. The programs are executed and controlled by a master control program known as the operating system. They consist of a suite or set of programs for validating, sorting, computing, updating and printing, etc. The sequential processing of each program in a batch processing environment is known as a computer run.

PURPOSE OF A COMPUTER

Production of Useful Information

The purpose of a computer may be defined as 'the accurate processing of data to produce information in the form it is required, at the right time, at an acceptable level of accuracy and at the right cost'. A computer when used effectively is a very efficient means of processing information and may be the central hub or focal point of information and accounting systems. They are capable of processing large volumes of data quickly and accurately. Large businesses will have large volumes of transaction data flowing through the system all requiring similar processing activities. This situation warrants the preparation of computer programs, or the purchase of package programs, for dealing with them (*see* Fig. 5.2).

Role of the Computer in Business

The role of the computer in business is no different in principle to that of any other method of processing business transaction data except that it does it faster and more accurately than a clerk using a manual

ELECTRONIC COMPUTERS: NATURE AND PURPOSE 47

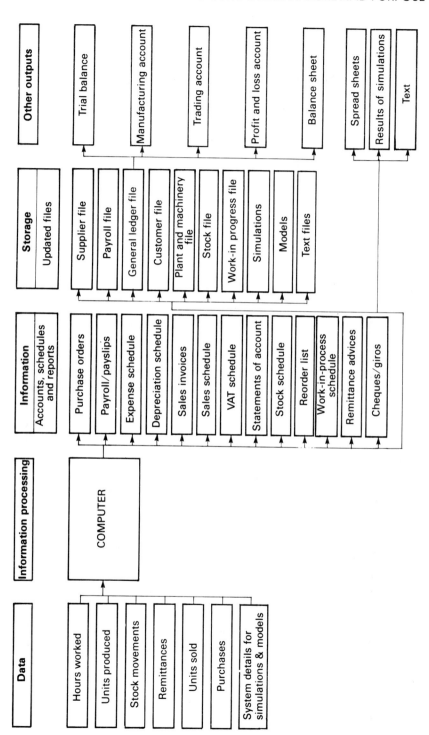

FIG. 5.2 *Computerised applications*

system. Large volumes of data are economically processed by computers, replacing the armies of clerks the larger businesses used to employ. Computers never suffer from fatigue as clerks do, however, they are prone to 'go down' or fail from time to time so they are not infallible.

Tasks for the Computer

The computer has many potential roles in business; it is capable of handling any application when the relevant program is loaded. The various tasks for which a computer may be applied includes:

1 Efficient and cost-effective processing of accounting data.
2 Administrative tasks, including the printing of purchase orders, processing sales orders and the preparation of reports for management control and decision making.
3 Solving statistical, mathematical, scientific and engineering problems.
4 Simulation and financial modelling, to help improve performance, i.e. techniques such as cash flow and break-even analysis, or optimising product mix for the purpose of minimising cost or maximising profit. Simulation provides a cost effective means of studying the effect of modifications on the behaviour of a system. Models of business situations may be constructed, such as the volume of sales anticipated at a defined selling price and the amount of variable costs and fixed overheads to be incurred in order to compute the projected profit from the operating data contained in the model. The model can then be modified by adjusting the various factors, i.e. the volume of sales or the selling price, and the 'What if' situation can be determined.
5 Project planning, i.e. discovering the critical path by means of network analysis. The utilisation of resources can be maximised with the aid of techniques such as linear programming and queueing theory, by means of specialised computer application programs.
6 Stock management; optimising stock holding costs, including interest payments on loans and the cost of storage.
7 Order processing, i.e. credit control enquiries may be made: the terminal operator can key in the customer account number and the program accesses the customer's record on the customer file and the operator can discover whether the customer's credit is satisfactory or unsatisfactory.

SUMMARY OF KEY POINTS

- A computer is a combination of related machines forming a configuration.
- A processor consists of three elements: arithmetic/logic unit, control unit and internal memory.
- A computer operates under the control of software known as an operating system.
- A program contains instructions which informs a computer of the operations to perform.
- Application programs are special purpose programs for specific applications.

SELF-TEST QUESTIONS

1. Why is a computer digital?
2. What is a computer configuration?
3. What is a processor and what does it consist of?
4. What is an operating system and what does it do?
5. What is a program and what does it do?
6. What purpose does a computer serve?
7. What is the role of a computer in business and what tasks can it do?

FURTHER READING

Data procesing 1, Principles and practice, R. G. Anderson, (6th edn) Macdonald and Evans/Pitman, London, 1987.

Information processing for business studies, A. E. Innes, Pitman Publishing, London, 1987.

CHAPTER 6
Selecting a suitable computer

LEARNING OBJECTIVES

This chapter provides a framework of how to select a suitable computer for the needs of a business. It emphasises the importance of conducting a feasibility study and of being aware of the benefits of computers in particular circumstances. The need to be aware of which factors to take into account in the choice of system, including cost factors, is stressed, as is the need to obtain tenders from selected manufacturers.

FEASIBILITY STUDY

We have seen how useful computers can be to all types of business. Before installing a computer it is usual to perform a feasibility study, to establish if the implementation of a computer would benefit the business in key operational areas. Businesses may consider the use of a computer for typical business systems such as order processing, payroll or accounting. The management decision to buy a computer is based on the facts obtained from the investigation, or feasibility study. A computer should be selected initially to suit current needs but it should be possible to expand and update it if necessary. Computers differ widely in size, speed, output capability and cost; it is necessary to select the most suitable combination of hardware and software for the proposed applications.

The gains from making the correct decision can be quite substantial but if the incorrect decision is made then the losses can be just as high. If it is decided not to implement a computer when one should be incorporated into the fabric of the business then business administration and accounting may not be so efficient. Implementing a large and expensive computer when one is not needed will lead to disenchantment and frustration, apart from being wasteful of scarce resources. The success of any computerised system will depend upon the attention to detail applied when assessing systems for which a computer is required, including identification of operational

SELECTING A SUITABLE COMPUTER 51

problems. It is therefore essential to discuss problem areas with relevant managers and operations staff; examine the forms and documents processed; the machines and equipment in use; the calibre of staff engaged on the various activities and company policy matters and the systems to which they relate.

Feasibility Study Report
A feasibility study report usually consists of four sections:

1 Machines and equipment (hardware) and software.
2 Staffing.
3 Operating costs.
4 Expected benefits.

Hardware and Software
It is necessary to consider the whole range of computers available, to choose one that meets the requirements of the business. Standby facilities must be available should the in-house computer malfunction, or to cater for exceptional processing volumes. Trends and projections regarding data processing loads will have an effect on the type and size of computer required. The availability of suitable software packages for the systems under consideration is of importance as this can save a great deal of effort on internal programming and systems development, and will enable systems to become operational sooner.

Staffing
The availability of experienced computer personnel is of prime importance. Existing staff may need to be retrained, and the organisation of departments or of work may need to be restructured.

Operating Costs
As a general guide large businesses, in terms of the volume of transactions they process, sales turnover and the number of personnel employed, require large computers because of their high speed processing capability. The cost of a large computer can run into millions of pounds, due to its speed, communication and multiprogramming prowess and its ability to support many terminals.

Expected Benefits
Medium size businesses can effectively utilise a powerful medium-size computer for processing smaller volumes of transactions

effectively. Small businesses may not be able to justify the cost of a medium-sized computer because of the smaller volume of transactions, but they may be able to think in terms of a small but powerful computer such as an IBM PC. Prior to the influence of the microchip on computing technology a small or even a medium size business often could not justify installing a computer because they did not process sufficient volumes of data to warrant such powerful processing facilities. Computers were also very expensive. Today, even the smallest one-person business could perhaps justify having a computer as they can now be employed in so many ways, and the cost has decreased so significantly.

VOLUME OF TRANSACTIONS

The number of transactions to be processed is an important factor to consider in the choice of computer because it is necessary to assess the type of input device required. Relatively low volumes of transactions can be effectively handled by a business microcomputer using a keyboard for the input of data. This is a slow method of data input, however, and would not be suitable for large data volumes. Where there are large volumes of data, multi user systems, where several people can use the same computer, at the same time, but from different terminals, are very helpful (*see* p.128). In such cases each user processes their own transaction data which means that payroll processing, invoicing and order processing can be performed concurrently. Real-time processing would also be performed using a terminal keyboard to input, update and retrieve data.

Business systems with thousands of records of different categories relating to stocks, personnel, customers, orders, suppliers and contracts, etc. require high capacity backing storage which should be capable of a high data transfer speed to and from the processor. Applications consisting of 500–1000 records may be suitable for processing by microcomputer using floppy discs which have limited capacity compared to that of hard discs, sometimes called Winchester discs. Some larger business microcomputer systems can have Winchesters added to their system for increasing the storage capacity and achieving a higher data transfer speed.

Use of benchmarks
Benchmarks are standard tests applied to different computers to compare their speed of operation and information processing capabilities. The benchmarks provide the time required to perform

different arithmetical processes and the time taken on other routine tasks such as sorting data into sequence and calling sub-routines from the main program. (Sub routines are sections of a program for performing repetitive tasks such as converting mixed numbers consisting of whole numbers and decimals into integers.) The timings provide a useful basis for selecting a suitable computer.

RELATIVE COSTS OF HARDWARE AND SOFTWARE

In the early days of computers hardware costs were extremely high but are now falling, mainly because of the revolutionary advances made in electronic technology: the size of computers has been reduced while their performance has increased. The cost of developing software on the other hand has a tendency to increase because of the labour intensive nature of the task. Some manufactuers provide *bundled* software, i.e. the cost of software is included in the total system cost. It is therefore essential to assess the total cost of any proposed computer system covering both hardware and software. If software packages are to be paid for separately then the cost must be added to the costs of the hardware. Only then can true comparative costs be formulated. It is, of course, necessary to assess the suitability of any bundled software packages as if they are not suitable for the systems it is proposed to run on the computer, then they have little value.

METHODS OF SELECTION

The relative strengths and weaknesses of different manufacturers' models must be assessed by comparing the specification of each selected model on a short list with the operational objectives to be achieved in terms of processing volumes and frequencies. For example, if a business has a large number of geographically dispersed offices, warehouses or factories then the number of communication channels a computer can control is of major importance. A *points rating* method of selection may be adopted whereby selected attributes are listed and points awarded from a maximum of ten for each attribute in the context of its utility to the business. A points league table may take the form outlined below:

1 Processor
   a Number of communication channels
   b 8, 16 or 32-bit processor
   c Memory capacity

d Number of peripheral ports for plug-in devices, e.g. serial or parallel centronic ports for printers, terminals and other devices
   e Speed of processor
2 Operating system installed
   Industry standard or otherwise
3 Software
   a Bundled or unbundled
   b Availability of suitable software for potential applications
4 Total purchase, lease or rental costs
5 Degree of manufacturers support
   a Installation support
   b Software support
   c Staff training services provided
6 Cost of maintenance agreement
7 Programming languages supported
8 Backing storage capacity
9 Multi-user/multi-tasking capability
10 Speed of printer
11 Other options

TENDER FOR CONTRACT

An investment in a computer system costing many thousands of pounds needs to be thought out very carefully. In such circumstances it is prudent to invite a number of reputable manufacturers to tender for the contract. The initial specification of requirements would typically include:

- Description of the system(s) to be computerised
- Volumes of data to be processed including frequency; minimum, average and maximum volumes
- Number of terminals/work stations required
- Geographical dispersion of operating units
- Multi-tasking and multi-user requirements
- Standby facilities required
- System priorities
- Real-time or on-line processing needs
- Nature and type of reports required, frequency of preparation and their distribution
- Maintenance contract considerations
- Extent of system support

Each of the manufacturers invited to tender would be supplied with the above details including flowcharts, organisation charts, document layouts and details of business operations. The details would be discussed by manufacturers' sales representatives with the systems staff and executives of the business. Discussions need to cover alternative proposals and configurations including their prospective costs and benefits. Management would then discuss all aspects of the proposals with their systems staff who will subsequently recommend the selection of a specific system.

PROPOSALS

The manufacturers' proposals should contain details about hardware requirements, software support, the type and duration of staff training to be provided, and the amount of systems support and equipment maintenance to be provided. Detailed cost schedules relating to hardware, software and the overall purchase cost should also be included in the proposals. It is important to consider the alternative financing methods available including purchasing, leasing or renting, before arriving at a final decision.

COST ELEMENTS OF A COMPUTER SYSTEM

Financial resources expended in the implementation of a computer need to be considered: a computer is a financial investment which must have an adequate return in the same way as any other investment in machines and equipment. No advantage is obtained or benefits achieved if costs are incurred to process data generating information which serves no useful purpose.

Capital Expenditure
Expenditure incurred in the purchase of computer hardware and software may be classed as capital expenditure, i.e. expenditure on assets which are not consumed in a single use. For accounting purposes it is necessary to depreciate computer hardware each year as its value diminishes. Costs incurred in converting an existing building or constructing a new building to house a computer is also capital expenditure but is not usually depreciated because the value of buildings usually increases. The costs incurred by installing air conditioning equipment, storage racks for tapes and discs and office furniture come into the same category. For a large computer installation it is usual to install a standby generator (again capital expenditure) which

can be switched into the circuit to avoid disrupting operations in the event of a mains power failure, and dust extraction equipment to avoid corrupting the contents of magnetic files.

Operating Costs
Computers incur operating costs during the course of daily routine activities. If a computer is purchased it will have annual depreciation costs; if a computer is leased or rented then it will have to be paid for accordingly.

If the premises housing the computer are not owned then rental charges will be incurred. Other establishment costs include local authority rates, building insurance, heating, lighting, office cleaning and electricity. The cost of private leased data transmission lines and of renting communication devices such as modems and multiplexors must also be taken into consideration, as well as insurance premiums and maintenance contracts, operating supplies, including magnetic discs, computer stationery, and standby computer bureau facilities. The cost of management and computer operations staff, including salaries, shift allowances and other payroll costs, i.e. pension schemes, National Insurance payments, etc. must not be forgotten. Further costs are incurred for staff attending training courses, telephone charges, travelling expenses, subscriptions to computer journals and so on.

System Development Costs
Costs incurred in *developing* computerised systems may be defined as 'once only costs', and include the cost of conducting feasibility studies, systems analysis and design, programming, changeover of files and, in the case of replacing an old system, running the two systems in parallel. Parallel operation is a 'fail safe' security measure which is required until the new system has proved satisfactory. Abnormal operating costs are incurred initially because of the need to employ additional staff and/or retain displaced existing staff for running the two systems.

SUMMARY OF COMPUTER ATTRIBUTES AND BENEFITS

Attributes
- High processing speed
- High degree of accuracy
- High capacity backing storage
- Data transmission facilities

- High speed switching between programs – multi-tasking
- Multi-access facilities enabling several users to share a central computing facility
- Internally stored program – immediate access storage.
- Automatic control of processing by a master control program – the operating system
- High speed print out of information
- Large capacity internal memory for the storage of programs and data
- Capable of being expanded on a modular basis
- Graphics capability
- Easy to follow menu displays

Benefits

- Improved cash flows may be achieved as a result of improved accounting systems, particularly credit control
- Random access facilities to information contained in databases, which may serve the needs of several functions
- Effective business control systems; the computer can compare related variables and branch to routines to deal with abnormal situations. Typical control systems include budgetary, cost, cash, credit, production and stock control
- More timely information flows as a result of high speed processing, which enables more effective decision making
- Both periodic (monthly) and annual final accounts can be prepared automatically, accurately, economically and in a shorter time by the use of integrated accounting packages.
- Increased processing productivity as a result of a computer's overall attributes
- Cost effective processing relative to the costs which would be incurred by manual methods
- Large volumes of data can be processed at high speed. This is particularly relevant to a mainframe, functioning automatically with a minimum of manual intervention
- Speedy retrieval of records for random enquiry purposes
- Built-in validation routines for the detection of errors, ensuring data integrity
- High speed transmission of data between geographically dispersed operating units
- Problem solving facilities by software such as spreadsheet packages
- Word processing capability

SUMMARY OF KEY POINTS

- The purpose of a feasibility study is to determine if a computer would benefit a business or improve the operation of a particular system.
- A feasibility study report contains details which enables a decision to be made whether to implement a computer.
- The relative strengths and weaknesses of different computers must be assessed to form a short list before final selection.
- A points rating method of selecting a computer may be useful based on various attributes.
- It is sometimes prudent policy to invite tenders for supplying a computer from a number of manufacturers.
- Manufacturer's proposals contain vast amounts of data relating to a proposed purchase of a computer.
- When considering the implementation of a computer it is necessary to assess capital expenditure, operating and system development costs.

SELF-TEST QUESTIONS
1. What purposes are served by a feasibility study report?
2. A computer should be selected initially to suit current needs but it is necessary to consider other factors. What are the other factors which should be considered?
3. Why is it important to consider the volumes of transactions to be processed before deciding on a specific computer configuration?
4. What method may be used to assess processing time for specific processes as a basis for appraising the performance of different computers?
5. What attributes would you include in a list to assist you in the selection of a computer?
6. What would you include in a specification of requirements for submission to a computer manufacturer?
7. What capital expenditure is associated with the installation of a large computer system?
8. What operating costs are incurred for a large computer installation?
9. Summarise the attributes of computers.
10. Summarise the benefits of using a computer in business.

FURTHER READING

The Penguin computing book, Susan Curran and Ray Curnow, Penguin Books, London, 1983.
The Guardian guide to microcomputing, Jack Schofield, Basil Blackwell, Oxford, 1985.

Part 4
The Mechanics of Information Processing

CHAPTER 7
File Order and Access Methods

LEARNING OBJECTIVES

This chapter outlines the mechanics of information processing in respect of file order and access methods. Included in this outline are the various ways in which files may be accessed on a serial access media and the various ways of obtaining direct access to records stored on magnetic disc.

SERIAL PROCESSING OF A RANDOM ORDER FILE

When records are not in any specific alphabetical or numerical sequence they are in *random order*. Such records can only be accessed in the sequence in which they are physically stored, by searching the file serially. Record number 1, for example, may be located midway through the file, record 50 at the beginning, and record 2 may be located at the end so the situation is counter-productive (*see* Fig. 7.1).

Logical and physical sequence do not coincide
Records accessed in physical sequence i.e. serially

R2	R5	R1	R3	R7	R6	R4	R9	R8

FIG. 7.1 *Serial processing of a random order file*

SERIAL PROCESSING OF A SEQUENTIAL ORDER FILE

After the transactions recorded on a random order file have been sorted by the key (reference) field it becomes a *sequential order file*. (*see* p. 31). As the master file is in sequential order, both the transaction and master files are compatible which simplifies and increases the efficiency of file updating (*see* p. 34 and Fig. 7.2).

Logical sequence of records in ascending order of key field
logical and physical sequence coincide

R1	R2	R3	R4	R5	R6	R7	R8	R9

FIG. 7.2 *Serial processing of a sequential order file*

DIRECT ACCESS

Indexed Files

Individual records are not stored in any particular sequence of key fields which means they are stored in *random file order*. Due to this random dispersion of records it is not possible to apply an algorithm for retrieving records. It is therefore necessary to generate an index indicating the location of each record.

Magnetic Disc: Indexed Sequential File

Records stored in sequential order on magnetic disc are recorded in ascending order of 'key' field. A random access storage device, such as a disc drive, avoids the need to search a file sequentially for locating a specific record. A cylinder and track index provides direct access capability (*see* p. 81 and Fig. 8.5).

When file activity is low, i.e. only a small proportion of the records on the file are accessed for updating or retrieval at one time, then direct access is more efficient than processing a sequential order file. This is one reason why disc files are more flexible and faster in operation than magnetic tape files which requires every record on the file to be accessed and tested to see if it is affected by transactions. The capacity of disc tracks is limited and they may get full preventing the insertion of records in their correct sequence. Such overflow records are stored on *overflow tracks*. It is important to maintain the sequence of records in the file and this is achieved by *chaining*, using link fields. By this technique a record which has been displaced into the overflow area has its new location recorded within the record which logically preceded it. The displaced record also has the location of the next record in logical sequence. This enables the sequential order of records to be traced. Access to overflow records is accomplished by a cylinder/track index which records the highest record key stored in the overflow area corresponding to each track indexed. The presence of the overflow address also indicates whether new records should be stored in the data area or the overflow area.

FILE ORDER AND ACCESS METHODS 65

FULL INDEX

An index record contains the disc sector reference for every record in the file. The file is sorted initially into key sequence and the index is constructed as the records are transferred to disc. The index is sequential but the records may be stored randomly.

PARTIAL INDEXING

Two or more levels of index are stored on disc. One level consists of a rough index containing the key (or reference number) of the last record in a specific range together with the 'bucket' location of the fine index related to that range. The rough index is usually transferred into internal storage during the time the file is in use. The rough index contains a cylinder number while the fine index refers to a specific sector on a specified surface in that cylinder. The records need to be stored in ascending key sequence in each bucket. Comparison of the key of the required record against the rough index specifies the cylinder in which it is located. The cylinder contains the relevant fine index as its first record. Reference to the fine index indicates the surface within the cylinder storing the record.

SELF-INDEXING

This type of file requires records to be stored in addresses that are related to their keys (reference number). File order is on the basis of a record address which is equal to its key. There are many variations of this because of differing disc starting addresses, different blocking factors (number of records transferred at one time as a block to and from the processor) and different structure of keys. Some key sequences have too many gaps to be organised in this way as it is inefficient in the use of storage. However, when it is possible to link the address and key of a record directly, self-indexing files are feasible.

ALGORITHMIC ADDRESS GENERATION

The basis of this method is a mathematical formula applied to the key of the record to be accessed from disc storage. The application of the formula generates a reference to the *sector* (section of the disc surface) storing the record. The sector is then searched to access the required record. It is then possible for the formula to produce the same address for different keys, creating an overflow situation necessitating several accesses to locate the desired record. Space is wasted when records are deleted from a disc file as the addresses will not be reassigned, because of the nature of the algorithm. The formal manner of establishing a suitable algorithm is to examine the key field sequence in use. It is then necessary to establish a formula which will generate an even distribution of addresses. Constants can be added to the formula to prevent unallocated storage locations and so avoid wasting storage space. It is essential to determine that the address is acceptable to the type of disc drive in use.

Algorithms are computed in a number of ways:

1 Random allocation of records is achieved by squaring the key, or part of it, and using some digits from the square, e.g. the centre digits, as an address. This technique can allocate more than one record to the same address and none to other addresses. The first record is stored in an address called a home record. If addresses can only hold a single record the subsequent records allocated to this address will have to be stored in overflow areas. These records are known as synonyms.

Example 1 Compute the address of the following keys by squaring the central two digits.

Keys:	5551	5552	5553
Digits:	55	55	55
Square:	3025	3025	3025

(to be used as an address)

It will be observed all records are allocated to the same address and are therefore synonyms.

Example 2
Compute the address of the same keys by squaring the last two digits.

Keys:	5551	5552	5553
Digits:	51	52	53
Square:	2601	2704	2809

It can be observed that gaps occur in the addresses of consecutive records.

2 Divide the key by a prime number and use the remainder as an address. This method will generally provide a good distribution of records. Sequence of keys produces remainders which do not generate synonyms as they each differ by 1.

FILE ORDER AND ACCESS METHODS 67

Before inversion

Customer	Attribute 1 Account balance £	Attribute 2 Credit limit £
1	5000	6000
2	4000	3000
3	5000	4000
4	1000	500
5	2000	1500
6	3000	2500
7	1500	1250
8	750	700
9	500	1000

↑ RECORD KEY

After inversion

Attribute 1 Account balance £	Customer							
0 – 1000	4	8	9	–	–	–	–	–
1001 – 2000	5	7	–	–	–	–	–	–
2001 – 3000	6	–	–	–	–	–	–	–
3001 – 4000	2	–	–	–	–	–	–	–
4001 – 5000	1	3	–	–	–	–	–	–
5001 – 6000	–	–	–	–	–	–	–	–

Attribute 2 Credit limit £	Customer						
Attribute 1 > Attribute 2	2	3	4	5	6	7	8

FIG. 7.3 *Inverted file*

Example 3
Compute the address of the following record keys by dividing the keys by the prime number 11 and use the remainder as an address.
   Keys: 5551   5552   5553
   Remainder: 7   8   9

A sequential spread of addresses is obtained which are acceptable.

INVERTED FILES

Inverted files are useful when no single key can retrieve a record, i.e. a combination of keys is necessary. The record is searched using a combination of keys known as attributes. Items possessing a specific feature are grouped together to form an inverted file. This reduces the time to retrieve records as it eliminates the need for serial searching. The keys and data are organised so that the keys (attributes) can be accessed one by one and only the relevant keys referenced (*see* Fig. 7.3).

SUMMARY OF KEY POINTS

- Records not in any specific order are in random order.
- After a random file has been sorted it becomes a sequential file.
- Records are sorted on a key field.
- An index is required to access records on a random file.
- Discs usually store indexed sequential files.
- A cylinder and track index provides direct access to indexed sequential files.
- When a disc track is full records are stored in overflow tracks.
- The sequence of records on disc tracks is achieved by chaining.
- Records may be self-indexing when they are stored in addresses that relate to their keys.
- The address of records may be compiled mathematically by algorithmic address generation techniques.
- Inverted files are used when no single key can retrieve a record because a combination of keys is required based on attributes.

FILE ORDER AND ACCESS METHODS 69

SELF-TEST QUESTIONS
1. What problems are encountered when serial processing a random order file on magnetic tape?
2. Why is it good practice to have records on tape in sequential order?
3. In instances when a computer configuration consists of both tape and disc storage facilities which type of storage would you select for an application with a low file activity?
4. What mathematical formula would you apply for algorithmic address generation?
5. Develop an example of an inverted file.

FURTHER READING

The Penguin computing book, Susan Curran and Ray Curnow, Penguin Books, London, 1983.

CHAPTER 8
File Processing

LEARNING OBJECTIVES

This chapter provides a knowledge of the mechanics of information processing with regard to sorting files and file updating including manual, magnetic tape and disc files and the methods applied to insert, delete and amend records stored on magnetic disc. The importance of the cylinder concept for access to records is also stressed.

SORTING FILES

The reason for sorting transaction data has been briefly covered in Chapter 4, and we will now look at it in greater detail.

Merge Sorting
This technique is used to sort large volumes of transactions stored on magnetic tape, but is also suitable for sorting large files on magnetic disc. The simplest type of merge sort is a two-way merge with fixed length strings. The essence of the method begins with a string one record long on a reel of magnetic tape; this is extended to two strings of records on two tapes followed by four strings of records on four tapes and so on, applying the technique of sort/merge until all the record keys are in ascending order (*see* Fig. 8.1).

Bubble Sorting
This technique sorts by successively exchanging pairs of records in the file and placing them in sequence. In effect the record with the smallest key bubbles to the top which converts the file into ascending order. If a pair of numbers is already in sequence the routine passes to the next pair and if the pair of numbers is not in sequence they are switched and the process continues in this way until the file is completely sorted.

	Pass 1		Pass 2		Pass 3		Pass 4		Pass 5
Input tape	Output tapes (input tapes pass 2)		Output tapes (input tapes pass 3)		Output tapes (input tapes pass 4)		Output tapes		
	A	B	C	D	A	B	C	D	
01	01	06	01	04	01	02	01	03	01
06	05	04	06	05	04	07	02	08	02
05	09	07	07	02	05	09	04	10	03
04	16	02	09	16	06	16	05	11	04
09	13	03	03	08	03	10	06	12	05
07	12	08	13	12	08	11	07	13	06
16	10	14	10	11	12	14	09	14	07
02	11	15	14	15	13	15	16	15	08
13									09
03									10
12									11
08									12
10									13
14									14
11									15
15									16
UNSORTED RECORDS									SORTED RECORDS

FIG. 8.1 *Merge sorting*

72 BUSINESS SYSTEMS AND INFORMATION TECHNOLOGY

Sorting Problems

Problem 1: Employee Records

A serial file contains approximately 10 000 employee records with the following format:

 employee number
 name
 age
 department (either Maintenance, Manufacturing or Marketing Department)

The records are initially in random order. Describe methods which will:

 a split the file into sub-files for each department
 b sort each sub-file into ascending order of employee number in each department

Assume that no more than 1000 records can be held in the main memory at any one time.

The solution has been provided in the modern idiom of defining the logic of a problem by the technique of Structured English. (Further details relating to Structured English are contained in Chapter 10.)

Solution:
 a Split the file into sub-files for each department:

```
OPEN FILES
WHILE (not end-of master file) DO
   READ master file
   IF (Department = Maintenance) THEN
      Output maintenance sub-file ELSE
   IF (Department = Manufacturing) THEN
      Output manufacturing sub-file ELSE
   IF (Department = Marketing) THEN
      Output marketing sub-file
WEND
```

 b Sort each sub-file into ascending order of employee number

```
*SPLIT INTO SORTED WORK FILES*
OPEN (sub-file AND 6 work files)
N=0
WHILE (not end of sub-file)
```

FILE PROCESSING 73

```
    REPEAT (until records = 1000 or end of sub-file)
      READ (sub-file)
    STORE (records in array)
    END REPEAT
    DO (bubble sort)
    N=N+1
    OUTPUT (sorted array to work file–N)
WEND

*MERGE SORTED WORK FILES*
A=1: B=2: C=6
WHILE (B not greater than N)
    READ (work file–A at end HV)
      (REM HV = high values)
    READ (work file–B at end HV)
    REPEAT (until end of both files)
      IF (record–A < record–B
    OUTPUT record–A
    READ workfile–A at end HV)
IF (record–B < record–A
    OUTPUT record–B
    READ workfile–B at end HV)
IF (record–A = record–B
    OUTPUT record–A
    OUTPUT record–B
    READ workfile–A at end HV
    READ workfile–B at end HV)
    END REPEAT
    B=B+1: X=C: C=A: A=X
WEND
```

Note:
Merges using the six workfiles are as follows:

   Workfile
   1–2–6
   6–3–1
   1–4–6
   6–5–1

Problem 2: Order and Customer Files
A manufacturing company makes a range of 20 different electric fires. Orders are input randomly in the following simple format:

74 BUSINESS SYSTEMS AND INFORMATION TECHNOLOGY

Customer code/product code/quantity required.

Prices, stock levels and customer codes are held on separate files. A discount of 10% is given on orders to the value of £400 or more and a further discount of 2% is given to special customers.

Describe a method to split the order file into two sub-files for special and non-special customers, and to sort each sub-file into customer code sequence.

Once again the solution is provided in Structured English style to provide an understanding of the logical aspects of the problem.

Solution:
  a Split the file into sub-files for each type of customer:

OPEN FILES
WHILE (not end-of master file) DO
   READ (order)
   READ (customer key=cust-code)
   IF (customer = special) THEN
     Output special sub-file ELSE
   IF (customer = non-special) THEN
     Output non-special sub-file
WEND
  Sort each sub-file into ascending
    order of code number:

SPLIT INTO SORTED WORK FILES
OPEN (sub-file AND 6 work files)
N=0
WHILE (not end of sub-file)
  REPEAT (until records=end of sub-file)
    READ (sub-file)
  STORE (records in array)
  END REPEAT
  DO (bubble sort)
  N=N+1
  OUTPUT (sorted array to work file–N)
WEND

MERGE SORTED WORK FILES
A=1: B=2: C=6
WHILE (B not greater than N)
  READ (work file–A at end HV)
    (REM HV = high values)
  READ (work file–B at end HV)

FILE PROCESSING

```
     REPEAT (until end of both files)
        IF (record-A < record-B
           OUTPUT record-A
           READ workfile-A at end HV)
        IF (record-B < record-A
        OUTPUT record-B
        READ workfile-B at end HV)
        IF (record-A = record-B
           OUTPUT record-A
           OUTPUT record-B
           READ workfile-A at end HV
           READ workfile-B at end HV
     END REPEAT
           B=B+1: X=C: C =A: A=X
     WEND
```

Note:
Merges using the 6 workfiles are as follows:

Workfile
1–2–6
6–3–1
1–4–6
6–5–1

b Describe a method to determine the income generated by each article.

```
REPEAT (until end of order file)
     READ (order file)
     READ (price file- key=product code)
     VAL = QUANTITY *PRICE
       IF VAL > 400.00
          INC G = VAL-(VAL * 10/100)
       READ (customer key equal customer code)
          IF (customer special)
             INC G = VAL-(VAL * 12/100)
       PRINT INC G
WEND
```

FILE UPDATING

The nature of files was outlined in Chapters 4 and 7. It was seen that records store details representing the current real-world situation of an entity; for example how much is owed by each of our customers, how much we owe each of our suppliers, how many items are in stock and which insurance premiums are in arrear. The master file is updated with transaction data which, in the case of stock items, includes issues from stores to production reducing the quantity in stock, and receipts or returns from suppliers which increase the quantity in stock illustrated as follows:

Brought forward stock balance		×
Add:		
receipts	×	
returns to store	×	
	——	×
		×
Subtract:		
issues	×	
returns to supplier	×	
	——	×
Carried forward stock balance		×

The updating process commences with an opening balance, referred to as the brought forward balance, and terminates with a closing balance, referred to as a carried forward balance, after a record has been adjusted with current transactions.

Some business applications do not require immediate updating of files as some high volume batch processing routines function effectively with only periodic file updating. In this case the files represent the status of the records at the date they were last updated. A factory payroll, for instance, is normally processed weekly because employees are paid weekly. Invoicing or billing routines may be performed cyclically according to the nature of the business. Gas and electricity boards update accounts of customers with the cost of the current quarter's units consumed, producing bills quarterly. Local authorities may produce rate demands once a year. Invoicing may be performed with any suitable frequency depending upon the volume of credit sales to be updated on customers' accounts in the customer file. Similarly, stock records may be updated daily to provide frequent information for stock management. In other instances, such as high stock turnover situations, then real-time control may be required necessitating the updating of stock records as movements

FILE PROCESSING 77

take place in order to be aware of the continually changing situation, thus avoiding overstocking and stock shortages (*see* on-line file updating, p. 12).

Example: Updating a Manual Sales Ledger
Figure 8.2 illustrates the updating of a manual sales ledger. The input to the updating process is a transaction file consisting of invoices. A clerk reads the account number of each invoice and selects the relevant customer's ledger card. The clerk records the invoice value on the ledger card, adds the value to the brought forward balance and

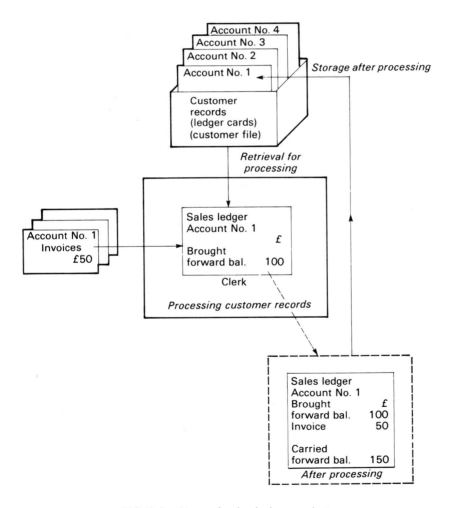

FIG. 8.2 *Manual sales ledger updating*

records the new balance, i.e. the revised amount owing by the customer (the carried forward balance). The clerk then refiles the updated ledger card. The process is repeated for each customer.

Updating Serial Files

Updating of records on serial files is carried out by pre-sorting the transaction file (*see* p. 63) allowing the key field of the records in the transaction file to be matched with the key field of the master file record. This enables a single pass through the file, rather than forwards and backwards searching. Records unaffected by transactions are written to a new file unaltered, but records affected by transactions are updated in the memory of the computer and are then written to a new reel of magnetic tape. Fig. 8.3 illustrates the processing of invoices which are to be recorded on the customer records for the purpose of updating them.

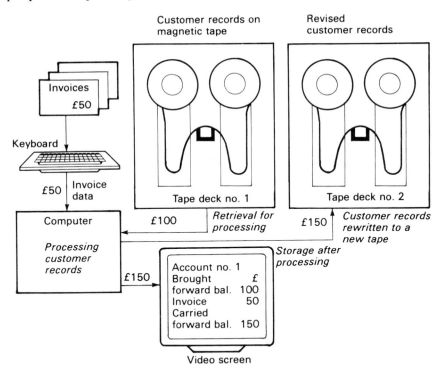

FIG. 8.3 *Computerised (tape-based) sales ledger updating*

Disc File Updating

Direct access is extremely useful for on-line processing applications as records can be accessed randomly from remote terminals located in the various branch offices. Some classes of information system are

FILE PROCESSING 79

categorised as real-time, on-line systems because disc files, capable of direct access to information, are permanently on-line to the computer. This means they are permanently connected to, and controlled by, the computer. Terminals are also on-line to the computer to facilitate the random retrieval of information stored in the files or to input data for updating the stored records. Such systems form an integral part of major business operations and it is essential that the stored information is representative of the actual status of the physical system. This requires the immediate updating of records as events occur. Examples of such systems include airline seat reservations, booking of hotel accommodation, theatre tickets and package holidays. Although these systems are dissimilar in nature, they are similar in that they have a stock of some commodity subject to critical control. Airlines have stocks of seats on different flights for various dates, hotels have stocks of rooms available on specific dates and theatres have stocks of seats for performances on certain days. Many terminals have simultaneous access to such systems, or so it seems – they are actually in a queue, and the status of information on the terminal screen visibly changes while being viewed. In this way the actual status of the system is immediately apparent and, what is more, the files are updated with bookings as they occur, thus preventing duplicated booking situations. Fig. 8.4 illustrates the updating of customer records by invoice values.

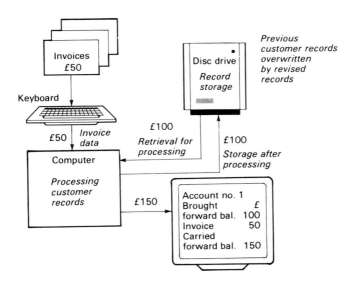

FIG. 8.4 *Computerised (disc-based) sales ledger updating*

The details which follow are based on a program written by the author. The procedure relates to updating a random file stored on a floppy disc on an Apple IIe microcomputer. The activity mainly revolves around the need to open and close files which are an essential part of the file access and updating program. The operator loads the required program by keying in the program name, e.g. LOAD STOCK. The computer searches the disc file, locates the required program and transfers it to the internal memory ready for further processing. A command prompt is then displayed on the video screen to which the operator responds by keying in the command RUN which executes the file processing program.

The program then requests the filename to which the operator responds by keying in the name of the file to be processed. The program then OPENs the relevant file and requests the number of records on the file, which is keyed in by the operator.

The program then CLOSEs the file and displays the message:

> THERE ARE N RECORDS IN THE FILE
>
> WHICH RECORD DO YOU WISH TO UPDATE?

The operator keys in the number of the record to be updated and the program reOPENs the file and READs in the required record. A message is then displayed:

> READING RECORD...
>
> QUANTITY TO ADD (or subtract)?

The operator keys in the relevant quantity: the program then adds the quantity and reOPENs the file and WRITEs the updated record to its original location on the same disc file. The file is then closed and a message is displayed:

> PRESS ANY KEY TO CONTINUE

The operator depresses a key and a further message is displayed:

> ANY MORE RECORDS TO BE READ?

The operator keys in Y for YES or N for No. If the response is Y then the program branches conditionally to the statement, and the following is displayed:

> WHICH RECORD DO YOU WISH TO UPDATE?

It must be appreciated that different computers require different program statements for file opening and closing. The above details demonstrate those for a specific computer and are outlined to provide additional information to the reader with an enquiring mind. Fig. 8.4 illustrates the configuration for on-line updating of a sales ledger. A keyboard operator reads the details on the invoices and keys the data into the computer where it is stored in the internal memory. A block of records is read into the internal memory of the computer from the disc drive. The record key of the transaction is compared with the record keys of the records transferred from the master file. When a transaction is matched with the relevant record it is updated. The illustration shows the account details on the video screen. The updated record is then written back to the same location on the disc when transferred to the disc drive. Only records with transactions are accessed: those without transactions remain unchanged and are not accessed.

Insertion of New Records on Magnetic Disc
When records on a disc file cannot be stored in the correct location on a track due to lack of capacity, i.e. when there is an overflow condition, the logical sequence of records can be maintained by using *pointers* and an overflow area. When a pointer is located the operating system retrieves the overflow record before dealing with the next in physical sequence.

Deletion and Amendment of Records on Magnetic Disc
Records can be deleted by physical erasing, and can be amended or updated by being overwritten.

Cylinder Concept
A cylinder is a notional concept rather than a physical entity; a conceptual cylinder is formed by a set of disc recording tracks on several disc surfaces. Some types of discs are known as *exchangeable disc storage*; these consist of several discs housed in a plastic container, known as a *disc pack*. The set of tracks which can be accessed by one setting of the read/write heads forms the hypothetical cylinder. As each track is concentric, the set of tracks represent the shape of a cylinder. The cylinder is referred to as the 'seek area' consisting of the number of records within the cylinder; this may comprise 22 concentric disc tracks in a disc pack of 12 discs. (The reason that there are not 24 tracks is that, although each disc is double sided, the upper surface of the first disc and the lower surface of the bottom disc are not used for recording data.)

82 BUSINESS SYSTEMS AND INFORMATION TECHNOLOGY

Using the cylinder is an effective way of accessing records as the continuous repositioning of the heads is eliminated. It is only necessary to reposition them to access a set of records stored in a different cylinder. Discs with 100 recording tracks for each surface provide 100 cylinders.

By means of a cylinder and track index, direct access to specific records is possible, facilitating random enquiries and on-line updating so essential to some operations. The computer first determines the cylinder in which a record is located, by means of the cylinder index which indicates the highest record key in each cylinder and a track index which specifies the highest record key in each track. The relevant track is then read to locate the required block containing the desired record. The block is transferred to the internal memory where it is searched sequentially until the required record is accessed (*see* Fig. 8.5).

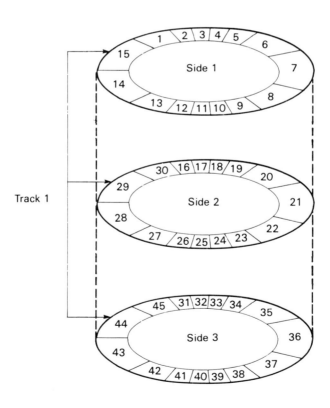

FIG. 8.5 *Cylinder concept*

SUMMARY OF KEY POINTS
- Merge sorting is suitable for sorting large files on magnetic disc.
- Sorting problems can be defined in Structured English.
- Files are updated with transactions so that records contain the current status of an entity.
- Some files only need to be updated periodically.
- Files in real-time systems are updated as events occur.
- Records stored on disc can be accessed randomly from remote terminals.
- When records are added to a disc file they are sometimes stored on overflow tracks.
- The logical sequence of records can be maintained in a disc file by means of pointers.
- Records on disc can be deleted by physical erasing.
- Records on disc can be amended or updated by overwriting the previous contents.
- The cylinder concept is an effective way of accessing records as the continuous repositioning of recording/writing heads is eliminated.
- Random enquiries are facilitated in on-line systems by cylinder and track indexes.

SELF-TEST QUESTIONS
1. What are the characteristics of merge and bubble sorting.
2. Why are files updated?
3. What circumstances determine if a file should be updated periodically or immediately events occur?
4. How would you update a manual sales ledger?
5. How would you update magnetic tapes files?
6. How would you update magnetic disc files?
7. How would you insert new records on magnetic disc files?
8. How would you delete and amend records on magnetic disc?
9. What is a cylinder and what purpose does it serve?

FURTHER READING
Data processing, 1, principles and practice, R. G. Anderson, (6th edn) Macdonald and Evans/Pitman, London, 1987.

CHAPTER 9
Information Processing Techniques

LEARNING OBJECTIVES

This chapter illustrates the mechanics of information processing in relation to the screen displays concerning the compilation of forms and the processing of records. The importance of developing an effective dialogue for communicating with a computer is stressed. A knowledge of the various types of dialogue including menu selection, use of command keys, natural language processing, fourth general language and interactive programming is also important. The use of icons, pointers, drop-down menus and windows is described.

DEVELOPING SCREEN DISPLAYS

Form Display

Many applications are designed to display the layout of a form on the VDU. The operator enters data into the appropriate boxes (*fields*) through the keyboard, the keyed-in details are recorded adjacent to the relevant field and the completed document is displayed on the screen. The print-out can then be used for its intended purpose, e.g. informing customers of items despatched or being invoiced to them. This sophisticated electronic method of processing documents emulates the preparation of forms by hand or typewriter. If clerks are to use computer systems they must become proficient in keyboard skills. Once the initial hurdle is overcome they will soon become familiar with the technique of displaying documents. Errors can occur when entering data initially but corrections are possible by re-entering data, and overwriting the previous entry.

When documents are to be prepared by this technique the system designer needs to take into account the number of characters that will fit across the screen, usually 80, and the number of lines down the screen, usually 24. Data fields should be located in a logical sequence. The left hand side of the screen can be designed to display data fields of a fixed nature such as names, addresses and account/code references. Transaction details are often entered adjacent to the relevant fixed field on the right-hand side of the screen. Several lines at the bottom of the screen are normally allocated for prompts such as a question asking if the details on the screen are correct or if there are any more items to be processed. The document on screen should show reference details, including the title of the screen, for example, order-entry screen, the name of the program to which the screen belongs, the originating author and the date of compilation.

Initial Display of Form Details
When the required program has been loaded and the command RUN is keyed in, the fields constituting a despatch note for informing customers of the goods despatched to them are displayed on the screen as shown below:

1. ORDER NO
2. CUSTOMER NO
3. DATE
4. DESP ADDRESS
5. ITEM CODE
6. DESCRIPTION
7. QNTY ORDERED
8. QNTY DESP

Data is input via the keyboard for each line of the display and the completed despatch note appears as follows:

1. ORDER NO   12345
2. CUSTOMER NO   567
3. DATE   12/12/87
4. DESP ADDRESS   12 SMITH ST. WALSALL
5. ITEM CODE   A1298
6. DESCRIPTION   BOLTS
7. QNTY ORDERED   60
8. QNTY DESP   50

The display is then printed out and sent with the goods ordered to the customer.

Display of Records when Setting up a Database
A database is a file of structured data. A particular set of records (data), such as asset records or customer addresses are entered into a database one field at a time. A database management system controls the structure of records, their amendment, addition, deletion, and display; it will search for specific attributes such as employees with weekly wages exceeding £100; and it will control the printing of

reports, etc. The details shown below relate to an asset record forming part of an asset register for accounting purposes. A summary of all the asset records in a database provides information for entering in a profit and loss account and balance sheet. The initial cost, field 5, is recorded in the balance sheet from which cumulative depreciation, field 7, is deducted, providing net book values. The total of the current amount for depreciation, field 6, is written off as an expense in the profit and loss account.

Fields	Content of fields
1. RECORD NUMBER	1
2. EQUIPMENT NUMBER	123
3. DESCRIPTION	CAPSTAN LATHE
4. SUPPLIER	ABC MACHINE CO LTD
5. INITIAL COST	£10000
6. DEPRECIATION	£1000 per period (year)
7. CUMDEPN	*

Field 7: Cumulative depreciation would be recomputed by the database software each accounting period to provide the cumulative depreciation to be entered in the balance sheet.

DEVELOPING DIALOGUE FOR INTERACTIVE PROCESSING

The Need for a Dialogue

Dialogue is the term used to describe the way in which computer users converse with a computer. A dialogue is, in effect, the means of interfacing the human element with the machine element of an information processing system. An over-simplified dialogue may not be acceptable to users as it may insult their intelligence. On the other hand a complex dialogue may be difficult to comprehend. Input errors are likely to occur due to misinterpretation or the incorrect use of dialogue. It is important therefore for the system designer to be aware of the status and calibre of the personnel who are to use the terminals/microcomputers. If the user is a computer specialist then they will be familiar with the dialogue used in a job control language and system commands necessary to achieve specified results. Dialogues need to be user friendly, guiding the user through the routines with the aid of explanations on the screen or references to the system manual.

MENU SELECTION

Many business applications display a menu for selecting alternative options, thus avoiding the need to type in messages or commands to

load specific files for processing particular routines. Options can be selected by:
1. Locating the cursor adjacent to the required option and pressing the Enter/Return key.
2. Keying in the number that specifies the required option – the number selection technique.

Menus may list the routines available to the user, as shown below alternatively they may list several applications from which a choice may be made.

1. Retrieve record
2. Update record
3. Add new record
5. Delete record
6. Print record
7. Print summary
8. End of session routine
9. End of period routine
10. File maintenance

Select desired option by keying in option number

COMMAND SELECTION KEYS

A dialogue consists of commands, which, in order to speed up entry to the computer, are abbreviated. A series of these abbreviated command options may be shown at the bottom of the screen when a program is being used. Details of the options are contained in the manual but as an example of their use, if option 'S' is chosen (the common abbreviation for SAVE) and the 'S' key is pressed, then the information keyed in up to that point is saved on disc.

NATURAL LANGUAGE PROCESSING

Knowledge Based System

Natural language processing comes within the sphere of artificial intelligence and is a means of communicating with a computer with the user's own language, whether it is English, Japanese, or whatever. The purpose of natural language processing is to simplify the use of computer applications for non-specialists thereby avoiding the need to learn operating system commands and computer languages. They also provide an interface to simplify the use of software by the non-specialist. Natural language messages are converted into the language of a specific computer, known as machine code, by a compiler which is a translation program. Natural language systems come into the category of artificial intelligence as they are knowledge-based systems. In order to understand a natural language enquiry, the computer must have built-in knowledge for the analysis and interpretation of the details input by the user. Before it can take action in response to the input it must have a built-in understanding of grammar, syntax, semantics, a complete vocabulary and the definition of words. The computer responds by generating a natural language output, achieved by built-in sentences, phrases and paragraphs. Applying the key word search technique the natural language processor program searches through a sentence for key words which have been input by means of a keyboard. Key words are then subjected to pattern matching by comparing them with words and phrases stored in the key word directory within the program. When a match occurs a built-in response is generated. It will be necessary to consider synonyms to allow for the different uses of specific words. For example, a computer instruction may also be known as a statement or command; goods sold and forwarded to customers may also be known as products, items or despatches. The use of key word pattern matching is restricted because of the problem of dealing with the variations in language expression. A superior and more widely applied technique designed to remove this problem is the analysis of the syntax and semantics of the details which have been input. This technique enables the meaning of an input to be more precisely defined. A problem still exists however because of the large number of words which have a variety of interpretations and the various ways in which they can be structured into sentences.

As an example of the use of natural language an accountant may require to know how the budgeted costs compare with actual costs in a specific department. The query may be stated in the following terms 'What are the budgeted overheads compared with the actual overheads for the sales department in September?'. The system will analyse the input and retrieve the relevant details from the database, compute the variances and present the details in columnar report format as shown below:

Budget and Actual Overhead Comparison Statement

Sales Department   Month: September

Overhead classification	Budgeted expenditure £	Actual expenditure £	Variance £

FOURTH GENERATION LANGUAGES

Fourth generation languages (4GLs) are non-procedural whereas typical computer programming languages are procedural. A *non-procedural language* is designed to assist the manipulation of a database. They specify *what* is to be done rather than *how*. Fourth-generation languages also include database management capabilities making a user-view of database operations transparent as the mechanics of how and where data is stored is the province of the database management system (DBMS). The primary purpose of 4GLs is to provide non-specialists, the end users, with the means to do their own information processing without having to become programming experts. A fourth-generation language translates the user's requests into procedural steps to produce the desired output. Most database management systems are integrated with a fourth-generation query language; this is a database user language providing facilities for creating, retrieving, updating, appending, deleting or amending data. A personnel executive may wish to know details of personnel in ascending order of age. Such requirements are formed into a question and the system performs the necessary computations, retrieves the details and presents them to the user. This is achieved with dBASE 11 commands, as an example, in the following way:

- USE PERSREV
- INDEX ON AGE TO AGE
- LIST NAME, AGE

If information is required about the weekly wage of personnel in ascending order of amount it can be obtained using the same query language as follows:

- USE PERSREV
- INDEX ON WAGE TO WAGE
- LIST NAME, WAGE

The reader should refer to the demonstration Creating and processing personnel records, Chapter 17, which provides several examples of using a query language.

The use of natural language is extremely useful when changing over from clerical to computerised applications as it enables personnel formerly employed on clerical operations to understand the new working procedures associated with computer operations.

INTERACTIVE PROGRAM

Many programs are designed to process data interactively, i.e. in conversational mode requiring a two-way communication between the computer and the user. Messages, often in the form of questions requiring a response from the user, are displayed on the screen; for example, 'Do you require to display another record?' or 'Do you require a printout?', to which the user responds by keying in Y or N. The program then branches to the relevant routine.

Example: Printing Invoices

A program designed to process and print invoices would display messages as outlined below:

Computer display	User response
INVOICE NUMBER?	The user responds by keying in the relevant invoice number. If the invoice number does not accord to a specified range then a message is displayed as shown on the left
INVALID NUMBER PLEASE REENTER	The correct invoice number is then entered
DATE OF INVOICE?	The user enters the appropriate date

Other messages are displayed using this type of dialogue.

ICONS, POINTERS, WINDOWS AND DROP-DOWN MENUS

Icons

An icon (or ikon) is a simple picture, or symbol, used on a VDU representing, for example, a disc, document, printer, diary or a calculator. When the calculator icon, for example, is selected by the operator the calculator program is automatically loaded into the computer's memory from disc, enabling the operator to perform calculations on screen.

Pointers

On some computer systems specific icons are selected by 'pointing' the cursor at the appropriate icon by means of a hand-held cursor control device, known as a *mouse*. On other systems cursor control keys are used to move the cursor, or pointer, to the icon (Fig. 9.1).

INFORMATION PROCESSING TECHNIQUES 91

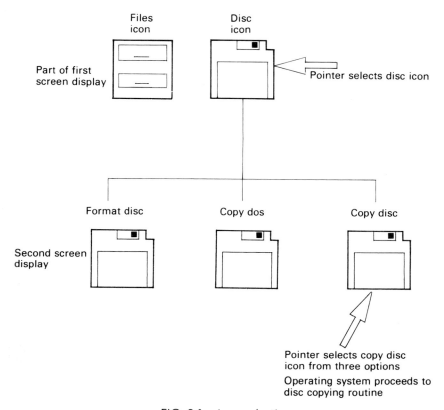

FIG. 9.1 *Icon selection*

Windows
If the operator locates the cursor over the disc icon, and pushes a button on the mouse, a window, i.e. a section of the monitor screen, will be displayed, listing all the files on that disc. The cursor can then be moved down the list of files to select the one required for processing. This is a speedy way of communicating with the computer, and is very 'user friendly'. The window acts as a viewing area of the computer's memory. In multi-tasking operations software may be used which allows windows to be opened for several tasks which can be viewed on the screen simultaneously. (For further details on multi tasking, *see* page 128.) The window may be closed when switching to a different task while the original task is being executed. Spreadsheet programs have facilities for displaying sections of a large spreadsheet, perhaps the top and bottom sections, simultaneously.

Drop-down Menus
Some computers use software which have drop-down, or pull-down, menus allowing quick and easy execution of commands. Using the

mouse, the operator can select an option from the display at the top of the screen, which brings down the menu from which the function, e.g. to copy a file, can be selected.

SUMMARY OF KEY POINTS

- Many applications display a form on a video screen to be compiled electronically.
- Records are initiated on a video screen when setting up a database.
- Dialogue techniques enable users and computers to converse.
- Dialogue techniques take many forms including menu selection, command keys, natural language, fourth generation languages, interactive programs, use of icons, pointers, drop-down menus and windows.

SELF-TEST QUESTIONS
1. Describe the characteristics of form displays stating their purpose and what method they supersede.
2. A dialogue is a means of communication between users and computers. State a number of important factors which must be considered in the design of a dialogue.
3. What purpose does a menu serve?
4. What type of dialogue is used when running a spreadsheet?
5. What are the features and purpose of natural language processing?
6. How would you define a fourth-generation language?
7. What features make a computer program become interactive?
8. Define the meaning of the terms icon, pointer, drop-down menu and windows.

FURTHER READING

Crash course in artificial intelligence and expert systems, Louis E. Frenzel, Jr., Howard W. Sams, 1987.

CHAPTER 10
Development of Information Systems

LEARNING OBJECTIVES

This chapter provides an appreciation of, and introduction to, the methodology of structured analysis and design for the development of information systems. The automated approach to systems development using Computer-Aided Systems Engineering (CASE tools) is described. The use of Structured English for providing a structured list of processes is outlined, as are the techniques of system flowcharting and prototyping.

STRUCTURED ANALYSIS AND DESIGN

The structured approach to designing information systems emphasises the solving of problems without technical constraints. A logical/conceptual model of a system is constructed specifying the requirements to achieve desired information flows and outputs (*see* Fig. 10.1). These logical needs are subsequently matched to the equipment during the physical design stage of system development. A logical model of the data flows is constructed and processes applied for transformation into system outputs. An efficient system development methodology is essential: it reduces the risk of wasting resources on systems development, increases the productivity of development staff by providing a standard method of developing each project, and provides the right tools and techniques for analysing and designing various elements of the system. The structured systems analysis and design method (SSADM) includes review procedures to enable errors to be identified and eliminated before system implementation. This method is widely used for systems development by the UK government.

A good method allows the system developer to accurately identify user information needs. At each stage management have a check list to review project progress, to assess what tasks should be completed and what deliverables are due. Long and complex narratives are replaced with graphical methods and Structured English, examples of

94 BUSINESS SYSTEMS AND INFORMATION TECHNOLOGY

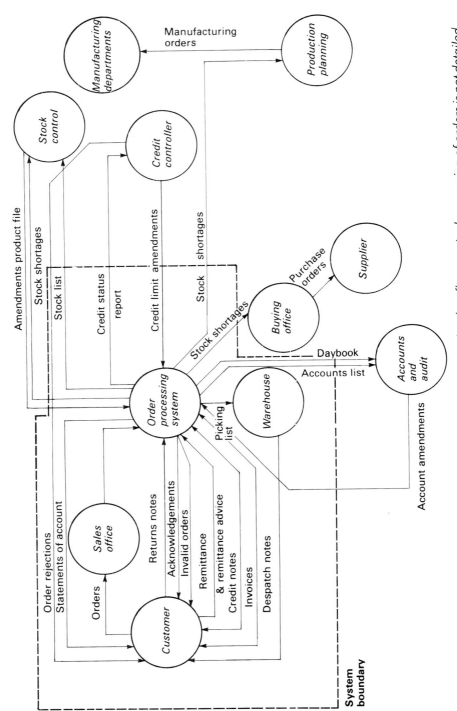

FIG. 10.1 Conceptual model of order processing system portraying data flows; actual processing of orders is not detailed

which are included in Chapter 8 and on p. 104. A data-driven top-down structured approach is often applied. This emphasises the use of data flow diagrams (DFDs), data analysis, data modelling and definition of processes by functional decomposition (these terms are defined below). The data-driven approach recognises that all applications have a data structure which does not change much over time, apart from routine amendments to data stored in files or databases. Most information systems are concerned with building data structures on conventional files or databases; accessing and extracting data from files and updating the file. On the other hand processes can vary due to developments in electronic technology – the impact of the microcomputer and local area networks, for instance. Structured methodology allows users to participate through all stages of development, and enable them to meet their specific requirements. It provides frequent walkthroughs, i.e. reviews which are designed to detect errors, omissions and ambiguities in any stage of development. The methodology provides for the checking of system logic during the analysis and design phases, instead of discovering them during the later stages of writing program specifications, program writing, program testing or during live running. Some proprietory systems of structured methodology, such as LSDM, also cover physical system design, including definitions of files or databases, programs and computer runs, resource usage estimation and optimisation.

Stages
The stages of the structured approach vary, according to circumstances and the nature of the business activity, but initially the same approach as organization and methods (O & M) analysis is adopted. The initial stages of O & M include collecting, recording, verifying and examining facts relating to the current system including details outlined in the following paragraphs. Whereas O & M tends to use procedure charts outlining the sequence of activities, the structured approach tends to use data flow diagrams and other techniques such as conceptual models as outlined below.

Terms of Reference and Systems Analysis
The terms of reference are obtained from management specifying the problems, strengths and weaknesses of the current system and what is required from the proposed system. The current system is then analysed for the purpose of becoming familiarised with: its characteristics; its purpose; the level of performance achieved; the data

96 BUSINESS SYSTEMS AND INFORMATION TECHNOLOGY

flows between sub-systems and departments; transformation processes; the nature and type of personnel; and the equipment used on the various processes and activities. This is the basis for the systems redevelopment into a much improved computerised system. Analysis also establishes the nature and identity of the various entities and their attributes including customers, suppliers, orders, products and departments, etc.

Conceptual Model
After the preliminary analysis stage, a conceptual model, a high level flowchart (*see* Fig. 10.1) is constructed showing: each entity and the relationships between them; the boundary of the system and its interfaces with other related systems; data flows in and out of the system; and the processes for the transforming of data.

Entity Life History Diagram
An entity life history diagram (*see* Fig. 10.2) is then prepared specifying the events which modify or update each entity's data. It is important to know what event (*logical transaction*) will trigger the creation of an entity. This may be a new record of an item to be added to a file (an insertion); an event that will change the status of the entity (an amendment); or an event which will eliminate it (a deletion). Stock records exist as long as the stock item is not obsolete. Such records need to be updated regularly in order to know how many items are currently in stock, on order and reserved for special orders or jobs,

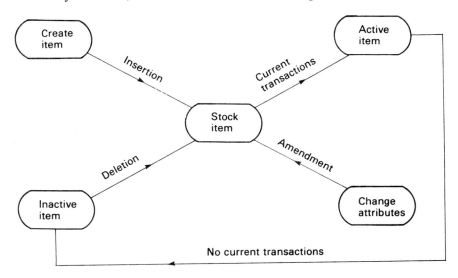

FIG. 10.2 *Entity life history for a stock item*

how frequently the maximum stock level is exceeded, and so on. Entity life history diagrams ensure that every entity has an event for its creation and deletion.

Transaction History Diagram
This is followed by the preparation of a transaction history diagram (*see* Fig. 10.3) showing how an entity changes with time – it represents transactions in chronological sequence affecting an entity within a particular system for example, for a stock record the nature of the various transactions will be shown, including items ordered, issues, receipts and returns, and details of receipts rejected – (either part of full order quantity), stock shortages, re-order levels and stock reserves, etc.

Context Diagram
A context diagram is a high level chart or block diagram which provides an overall view of the system showing the primary inputs, data flows in and out of files, and outputs. An example relating to a payroll system is illustrated in Fig. 10.4. A context diagram provides an initial overview of the data flows in a system and is used as a basis for developing more detailed data flow diagrams, discussed below (*see* Fig. 10.3).

Data Flows
The data elements (*attributes*) relating to each input data flow are then specified, an essential requirement for the subsequent design of forms and data modelling, and a prerequisite to the design of file structures. Data elements (attributes) of output data flows and the origins of data flows are established, supplemented by the preparation of a data flow diagram.

Data Flow Diagram
A data flow diagram (DFD) provides a visual representation of the elemental structure of a system including entities, processes, data flows and data stores (files), illustrated in Fig. 10.5. DFDs can be used to show both broad and detailed data flows. The high level data flows, outlining the system in very broad terms, are subjected to the process of partitioning or levelling for the purpose of obtaining increasing levels of detail. This process is repeated to the ultimate level of detail, known as a *functional primitive*. A data flow diagram shows how data moves through a system. They should be plotted in the sequence in which they occur, in order to provide an extension to

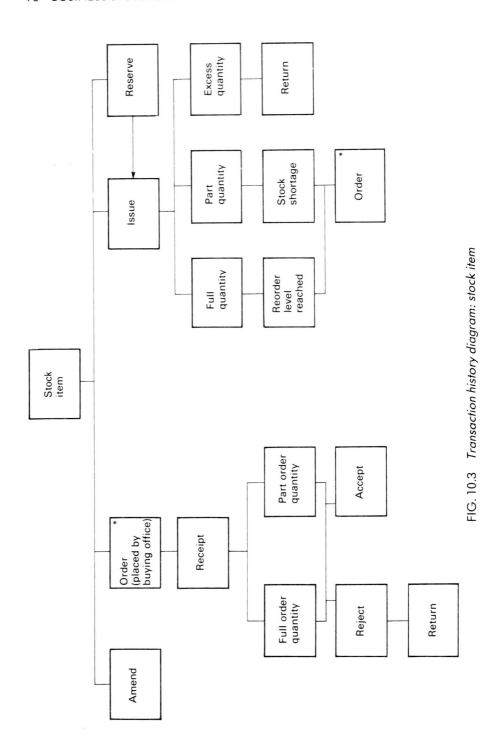

FIG. 10.3 Transaction history diagram: stock item

DEVELOPMENT OF INFORMATION SYSTEMS 99

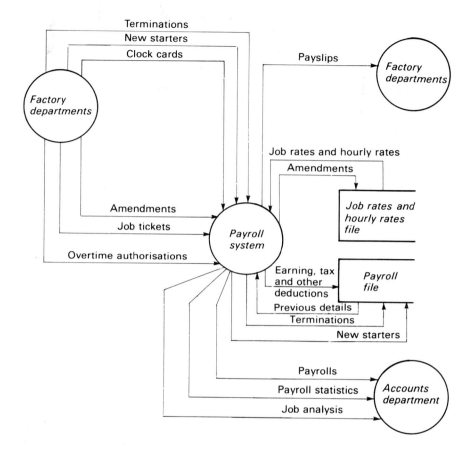

FIG. 10.4   *Context diagram of payroll system*

the logical approach and subsequently save valuable time when constructing a system flowchart of the logical structure of a system. Most of the details required to develop a new system can be summarised in a data flow diagram which may dispense with the need for a detailed supporting narrative, (such a narrative is essential when using system flow charts).

Data Modelling and Entity Diagram

Data modelling is then undertaken, using an entity diagram showing relationships between data items, their entry points and access paths. Fig. 10.6 illustrates the entity relationships in a typical stock control system showing the flow of information from source to destination and the type of relationship. For example, 'many-to-many' transactions; many delivery notes are received in the stores from many

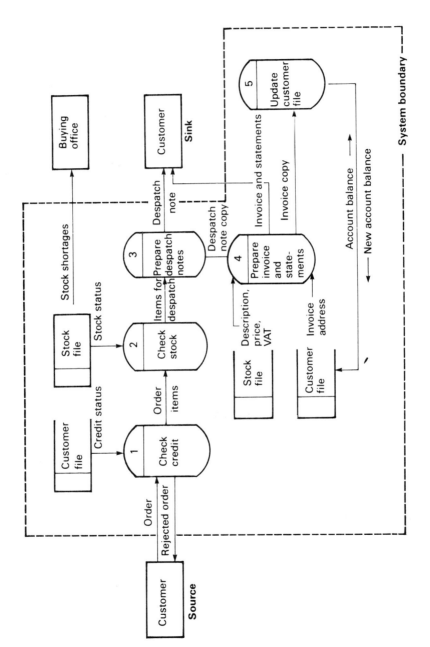

FIG. 10.5 Simplified data flow diagram: order processing

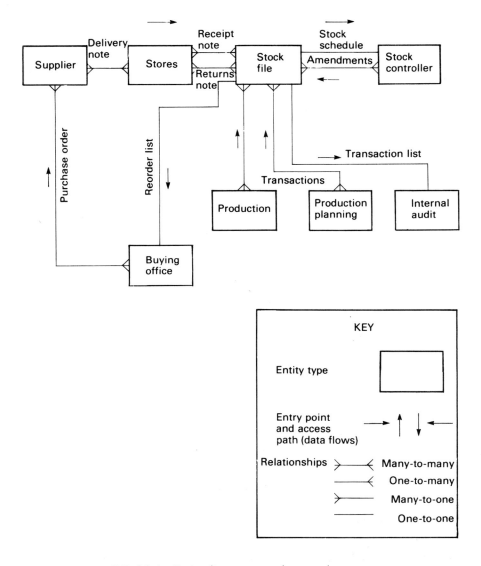

FIG. 10.6 *Entity diagram: stock control system*

suppliers: many purchase orders are sent from the buying office to many suppliers.

Functional Decomposition

A decomposition diagram (*see* Fig. 10.7) is then prepared which analyses high level definitions of a function, into more detailed functions for further analysis. The decomposition diagram of this refinement process forms an inverted tree structure.

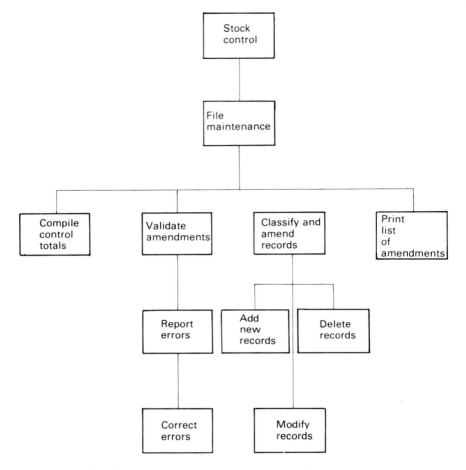

FIG. 10.7 *Functional decomposition – File maintenance*

System Flowchart

A system flowchart or run chart is then constructed, outlining the logical features of the system, and used as a basis for assessing the physical design requirements of the information system (*see* Fig. 10.8). When the machine and technical options have been considered an initial flowchart of the physical system is prepared, referred to as the *first sketch*.

SUMMARY OF THE STAGES OF THE STRUCTURED APPROACH

1 Obtain terms of reference.
2 Analyse current system including data analysis.
3 Construct conceptual model.

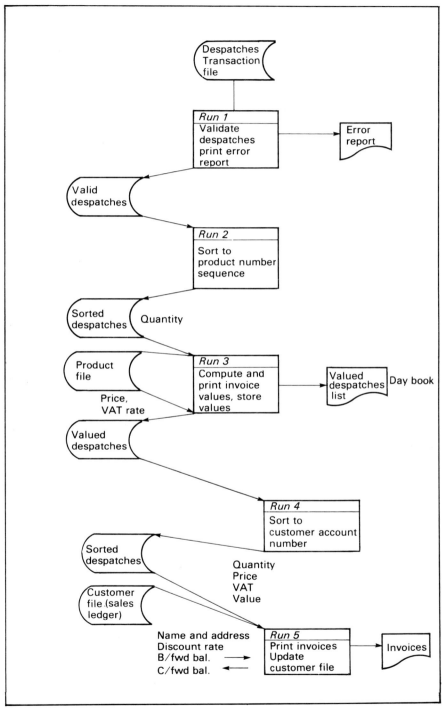

FIG. 10.8 *Run chart: disc-based batch processing invoicing and sales ledger application*

4 Analyse entity life and transaction histories.
5 Construct context diagram.
6 Specify data elements (attributes) relating to each input data flow. Specify data elements (attributes) of output data flows and the origin of each output data flow.
7 Specify input and output data flows and an outline of processing activities by means of a comprehensive data flow diagram.
8 Transform analysis-levelling of data flows.
9 Data modelling using an entity diagram to depict the relationship between data items, their entry points and access paths.
10 Functional decomposition of processes.
11 Construct flowchart portraying logical model of the system.
12 Initial flowchart of physical system – first sketch.

AUTOMATED APPROACH TO SYSTEMS DEVELOPMENT – COMPUTER-AIDED SYSTEMS ENGINEERING (CASE)

Businesses today must take every opportunity to develop efficient and effective information systems to accomplish a defined level of performance, quality assurance, speedy access to information, and cost effective system operation. In order to achieve these goals and improve the productivity of systems development automated methodology should be implemented using CASE tools, i.e. Computer-Aided Systems Engineering, which replaces the old fashioned method of pencils and plastic flowchart templates. This reduces the time required for systems development and results in superior quality computer systems. The user therefore has quality assurance and acceptable deliverable outputs and the management and systems developers obtain the benefits of increased productivity.

Advantages of CASE tools

- development productivity increased
- development costs have a shorter pay-back period
- quality assurance improved
- deliverable outputs in a shorter time period

STRUCTURED ENGLISH

Structured English is a useful technique for specifying the logic of a problem when developing information systems. The syntax of Structured English is limited and omits most punctuation, all adjectives and all adverbs. It consists of a combination of English words and program-type instructions and is used to define the logical processes of a system.

Example: Customer Discount
This example relates to the computation of customer discounts based on two factors: order value and the account balance. The specific details are evident within the details provided in Structured English.

1. Read customer order
2. Assess order value
3. Assess account balance
4. Compute discount
5. Repeat processing of transactions until completed
6. Print control totals
7. End

The actions converted into Structured English are as follows:

    READ customer order
    WHILE (not end of transactions) DO
       IF (order value is less than £100 AND account balance is less than £500) THEN
           Compute discount at 2% ELSE
         IF (order value is greater than £100 AND account balance is less than £500) THEN
           Compute discount at 3% ELSE
         IF (order value is greater than £100 AND account balance is greater than £500) THEN
           Compute discount at 1% ELSE
         IF (order value is less than £100 AND account balance is greater than £500) THEN
           No discount is provided
         REPEAT UNTIL (not this customer order)
         READ customer order
      PRINT control totals
      ENDDO

Characteristics of Structured English
Structured English has a limited vocabulary consisting of imperative verbs to express functions; data dictionary terms including nouns for the name of data items, documents or reports, and reserved words for logic formulation.

Three Structures

Pseudocode incorporates three structures – sequence, selection and repetition – or iteration – each are outlined below.

Sequence

Each action follows the next as specified in a computer program.

Selection

A control structure allowing tests to be made for conditions using the IF THEN ELSE construct.

Repetition (iteration)

Repetition or iteration continues as long as a condition remains true. It utilises loop statements such as WHILE DO or WHILE WEND. REPEAT UNTIL.

The number of conventions need to be considered when applying Structured English. These include:

1 Selection control structures using IF-THEN can dispense with ELSE when a condition can only have one possible action to deal with it.

2 An iteration can repeat an activity a specified number of times or until a file or transactions are completely processed.

3 The completion of an iteration structure should be terminated with an ENDDO or other similar convention.

4 Parentheses should be used abounding conditions when using IF or WHILE statements.

5 Subordinate sentences should be indented for purposes of clarity.

FLOWCHARTING INFORMATION SYSTEMS

Flowcharting Technique

Flowcharting is a technique for representing the features and characteristics of a system diagrammatically. Flowcharts facilitate the effective development of systems and are useful for providing an overall pictorial view of a system. Standard symbols are used for the construction of flowcharts which represent: various types of hardware device and/or processing activity including input devices; the type of input such as magnetic tape or disc; an action box specifying the nature of the computer process; storage devices with symbols which also indicate the nature of the files used in each run (*see* Fig. 10.8 and 10.9).

Block Diagram

A block diagram, sometimes referred to as a 'system outline' or 'system function' diagram is a low level flowchart which portrays the

DEVELOPMENT OF INFORMATION SYSTEMS 107

whole of a system in simple terms. It indicates the inputs, files, processing and outputs independent of operation details. An example is provided in an Fig. 10.10 which illustrates an order processing system.

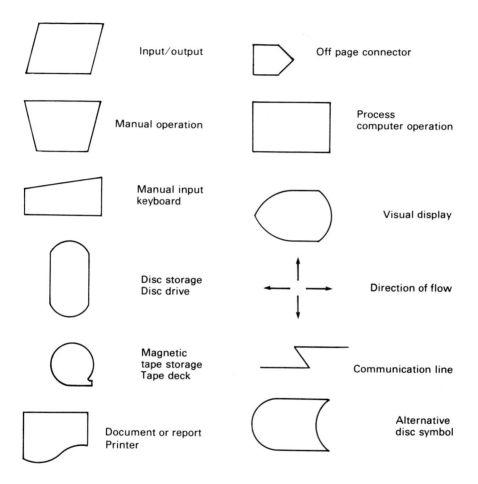

FIG. 10.9 *Flowcharting symbols*

System Flowchart

A system flowchart (run chart) is a pictorial or symbolic representation of a system. In its widest sense the term is used to describe any type of diagram showing the functions, data flows and the sequence of events or activities in a system. It includes both computerised and non-computer operations and also portrays the type of devices used such as disc or tape drives (*see* Fig. 10.8 and 10.11).

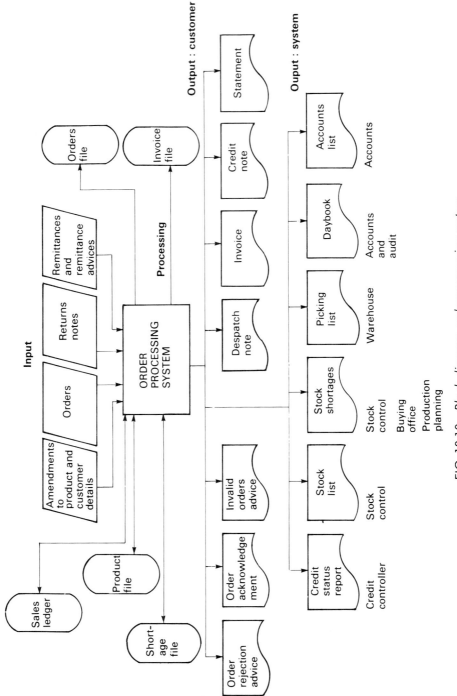

FIG. 10.10 *Block diagram order processing system*

DEVELOPMENT OF INFORMATION SYSTEMS

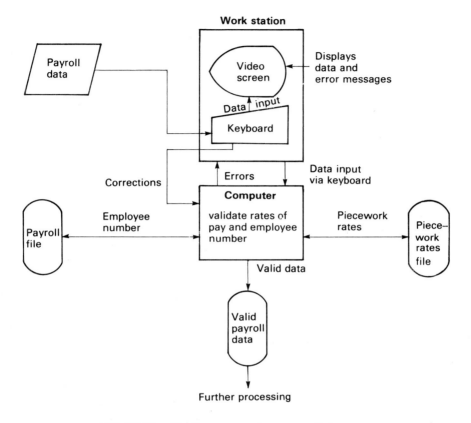

FIG. 10.11 *On-line processing: payroll data entry*

Applications to be portrayed on a flowchart usually consist of various combinations of standard processes, which may be summarised as follows:

1. Data recording on source documents.
2. Data capture by factory data recorder or laser scanning.
3. Date conversion, i.e. encoding by tape encoding or key-to-disc system.
4. Data verification.
5. Data validation.
6. Sorting.
7. Computing.
8. Comparing variables and parameters.
9. Updating files.
10. Printing reports and documents.

Computer Run Chart

Computer run charts are a specific type of flowchart for portraying the different runs performed on a computer including data inputs, processing operations and outputs from each run. A run chart provides the computer operator with information about the hardware devices required for each run, by means of appropriate symbols. Each run is shown separately with a brief narrative specifying the activities performed and its relationship with other runs. Fig. 10.8 is constructed vertically, progressing through the various tasks until the job is completed. A flowchart commences with an input of data which may come from a disc file prepared on a key-to-disc system; a floppy disc; a reel of magnetic tape; or a keyboard during on-line entry applications (*see* Fig. 10.11). The action boxes represent the activity performed by the computer. The result of processing often produces an output of information which consists of details of transactions to be printed on appropriate documents, and updated records which are to be recorded on a disc or tape file. Appropriate symbols are used for this purpose. (*See* Fig. 10.9.)

Summary of Rules for the Construction of Runcharts and System Flowcharts

1. Dated to identify the period of time to which flowchart relates.
2. Titled to identify the system portrayed by the flowchart.
3. Person originating the flowchart should be named.
4. Standard symbols should be used. *See* Fig. 10.9.
5. Rough sketch prepared initially to establish system logic.
6. Drawing aids should be used.
7. Logical sequence of activities should be portrayed. *See* Fig. 10.8.
8. Nature of processing should be stated whether manual, batch or on-line. *See* Fig. 10.11.
9. A run chart should only show processes performed by the computer. *See* Fig. 10.8.
10. A system flowchart shows all types of processes and activities including clerical support operations such as data recording, encoding and batching.
11. Frequency of processing should be stated as all processes of the same application are not always carried out with the same frequency. Some processes are daily, others weekly, etc. *See* Fig. 10.12.
12. Commence with an input. *See* Fig. 10.13.
13. Terminate with an output or filing process. *See* Fig. 10.13.

DEVELOPMENT OF INFORMATION SYSTEMS

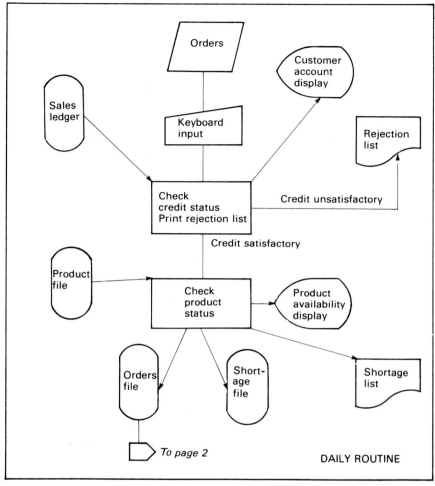

FIG. 10.12 *Integrated order processing system: on-line processing Integrated order processing system: batch processing*

14 Vertical presentation from input to output. *See* Fig. 10.8 and 10.12.
15 Output from one run may be the input to the following run. *See* Fig. 10.12.
16 The flow of information should be clear.
17 A legend should be used to describe input and output in general terms. *See* Fig. 10.14.
18 Off-page connector should be used for continuity from one page to another. *See* Fig. 10.12.
19 Narrative applied to briefly describe each process. *See* Fig. 10.14.
20 Number each run for reference purposes. *See* Fig. 10.12.

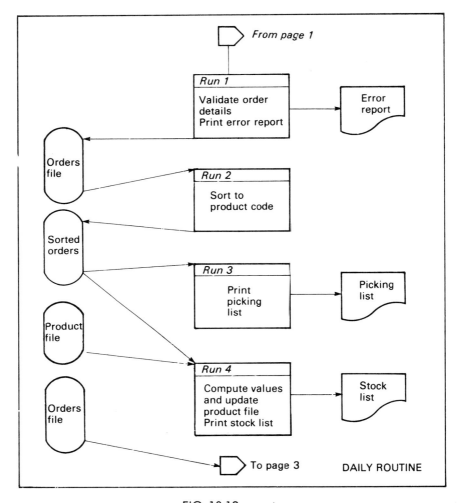

FIG. 10.12 cont.

PROTOTYPING

Prototyping is a technique used for building a model of a proposed system for the purpose of demonstrating to users how it can achieve their information needs. Fourth-generation software can be used to develop forms-based applications quickly and easily. The software acts as an interactive applications generator using pop-up menus, windows and screen painting to help users design, build and modify forms-based applications for integration with a database. Instead of programming an application it is developed by making menu choices allowing non-technical users to develop their own systems. The

DEVELOPMENT OF INFORMATION SYSTEMS

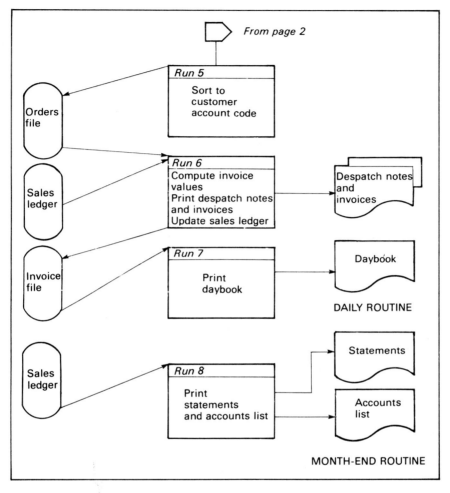

FIG. 10.12 *cont.*

software automatically handles all routine forms operations – insert, update, delete and query – without requiring the user to write a line of programming code.

Initially a prototype form is developed which may be improved by users in accordance with their needs and knowledge of the system. The model incorporates details of business transactions and the records to be used. As changes are specified they are quickly incorporated into the application. If the user finds the prototype unacceptable due to inconsistencies, omissions or other weaknesses then these matters are subjected to further discussion. Once the prototype model has been approved it can be implemented as the physical sys-

114 BUSINESS SYSTEMS AND INFORMATION TECHNOLOGY

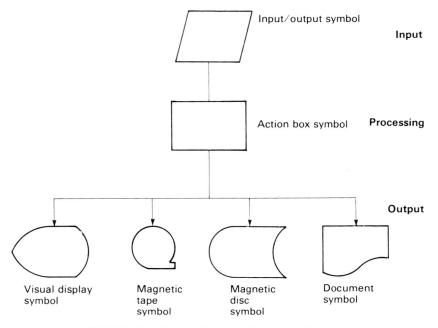

FIG. 10.13 *System flowcharting: use of symbols*

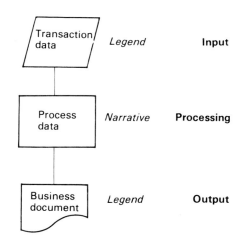

FIG. 10.14 *System flowcharting: use of legends and narratives*

tem. Alternatively it may be used as a system specification for the design of a working system.

The software is non-procedural so it is a simple matter to modify the model. Prototyping describes a system to users by letting them experiment with how it functions instead of providing them with a detailed written description which they may not readily understand.

After trying fully operational prototypes, users can suggest improvements in function and layout. New applications are easily implemented with this system whereas traditional development methods take much longer.

SUMMARY OF KEY POINTS

- The structured approach is widely used for developing information systems.
- A top-down approach is often used to develop systems.
- Data flow diagrams are useful for system development.
- Terms of reference provide the framework for conducting system investigations.
- A variety of diagrams and models are used for systems analysis and development.
- Computer-Aided Systems Engineering (CASE)—the automated approach—is becoming widely applied.
- Structured English is a useful technique for specifying the logic of a problem.
- Flowcharting is widely used to portray system features.
- Prototyping is a technique for building a model of a proposed system.

SELF-TEST QUESTIONS
1. What is the structured approach to systems development?
2. List the stages of structured analysis and design.
3. What are Terms of Reference and why are they required?
4. Define the terms conceptual model, entity life history diagram, transaction history diagram, context diagram, data flow diagram, data modelling and entity diagram, functional decomposition, system flowchart.
5. What is Computer-Aided Systems Engineering?
6. State the purpose of Structured English and outline its characteristics.
7. What is the purpose and nature of flowcharting?
8. Summarise the rules for constructing system flowcharts.
9. What is prototyping?

FURTHER READING

Practical systems design, Alan Daniels and Don Yeates, Pitman Publishing, London, 1986.

Business information systems, Chris Clare and Peri Loucopoulos, Paradigm, London, 1987.

Systems analysis, design, and development with structured concepts, Perry Edwards, Holt-Saunders, 1985.

Structured systems development techniques: strategic planning to system testing, Garfield Collins and Gillian Blay, Pitman, London 1982.

Part 5
Computer Applications – 1

CHAPTER 11
Computer Hardware and Processing Methods

LEARNING OBJECTIVES

This chapter provides an appreciation of computer hardware; processing methods and techniques including the characteristics of batch processing for large volume processing requirements; and details of the type of configuration required including input, storage and output devices and communication equipment.

SELECTION OF PROCESSING METHOD

Before it is possible to establish the configuration, i.e. the type and size of computer, input, storage and output devices required for the jobs to be computerised, it is necessary to know what processing method is to be employed. This will depend upon the nature and characteristics of the various applications being considered for processing by computer. Important factors will include an assessment of the volume of transactions and the required frequency of processing, as well as the importance of dealing with transactions as they occur. For example, if a job requires high volumes of transactions to be processed then it is appropriate to consider a batch processing application. If, on the other hand, it is necessary to input transactions and update computer files as events occur – for example, building society and bank branch operations, then interactive on-line processing is required. There are other processing methods to consider which will be discussed later in the text. Having decided on the type of processing needed to achieve the processing objectives of specified business applications it is then possible to establish the type of computer configuration best suited to these requirements. Before attempting this, however, the nature of batch processing will be defined and analysed.

BATCH PROCESSING CHARACTERISTICS

This method processes transactions in batches at predefined intervals of time. The method is suitable for frequent processing of large volumes of data. Significantly, batch processing is a semi-automatic and economical technique; it is semi-automatic because it needs an operator to handle files, load the printer with appropriate stationery and monitor the system's performance; it is economical because data is transferred from storage devices at high speed and processed internally at speeds measured in millions of instructions per second (MIPS) in some instances. It may be contrasted with a mass production semi-automatic manufacturing system which processes materials through a series of consecutive operations until the item is ready for despatch. A batch processing application is structured as a series of consecutive sequential processes known as 'runs'. Each run deals with a specific stage of processing through which all the transactions pass in a batch, before the next run is initiated. Each run has its own program. A computer operator places the disc file on which the program is stored onto a disc drive for transferring the program to the internal memory where it must be resident before processing can commence. This is referred to as 'loading' a file. The operator then selects the transaction file relevant to the application to be processed, for example, despatches to customers, factory wages data, or stock transactions for the previous week. The relevant master file to be updated by the transactions is also selected and both the transaction and master file are placed on the relevant storage device.

Batch Processing Application – Invoicing and Updating a Sales Ledger
The following example will outline the routine for preparing invoices and updating specific customers' accounts in the sales ledger from the input of details of items despatched to customers. The processing details are also shown on a flowchart, *see* Fig. 10.8.

Data is initially recorded on despatch notes in the warehouse from details of customers' orders, which typically include the following details:

Customer Order
Data elements
- Customer account number
- Customer order number
- Date of the order
- Code number of each item ordered (item code or product code)

- Description of each item ordered
- Quantity of each item ordered

The despatch details recorded on the despatch notes need to be converted into a format that the computer can understand; the data must be recorded (encoded) to magnetic disc to allow data to be transferred into the processor from the disc drive automatically, at high speed. *Encoding* is a data preparation activity which uses a keyboard encoding machine to convert data from handwritten details (as recorded on the despatch note) to binary code – the language of the computer. The computer then carries out invoice computations as directed by the set of programs, known as a *suite* of programs, by means of the processor's arithmetic/logic unit.

Processing Runs

Run 1: Input and validate despatch details.
 This ensures that the details of despatches, previously recorded on a disc transaction file, contain the correct data and that the quantities despatched are not abnormal. Despatch notes containing errors (invalid data) have the relevant details printed on an error report so that they may be corrected and represented for processing. Valid details are output (recorded) to a disc file for further processing.

Run 2: Sorting to product code.
 Despatches are sorted into the sequence of the product file, i.e. product code number sequence. Sorting of transactions is performed on specified parameters (reference fields) by a sorting program known as a utility program.

Run 3: Compute invoice values and print daybook.
 The output from run 2 is input to this run together with product prices and VAT rate from the product file. The program then computes invoice values and stores them on a valued despatches file for input to run 4. A complete listing of all the invoice values is produced which is the equivalent of a daybook in a manual accounting system. The listing is also used as an audit trail which enables auditors to trace transactions through the system from the input of despatch details to the printing of invoices and updating the sales ledger.

Run 4: Sorting to customer account number.
 The transactions on the valued despatches file are sorted to cus-

tomer account number so that they can be matched with the relevant customer record.

Run 5: Print invoices and update customer accounts (sales ledger).
The sorted, valued despatches file is input together with the sales ledger file (customer file). Name and address details and discount rate are printed on the invoice from the sales ledger file and quantities and prices, etc. from the despatches file. The accounts of customers are updated in the memory of the computer before being transferred back to disc, providing an up-to-date status of each account showing how much is currently owed by each customer and an age analysis of the total amount for credit control purposes.

```
              Updating process
    Brought forward account balance       ×
    add:
    Invoice value                         ×
                                         ___
    Carried forward account balance       ×
```

The content of a typical invoice is listed below.

Invoice
Data elements:

- Name of document
- Name of business
- Invoice number
- Invoice date
- Customer order number
- Invoice address
- Delivery address (if different from invoice address)
- VAT registration number
- Terms of payment
- Item code
- Item description
- Quantity (from despatch notes)
- Price (from product file)
- Value (computed)
- Discount %
- Discount amount (computed)
- Net invoice value (computed)
- VAT %

- Carriage/post charge
- Invoice net total (computed)
- VAT total (computed)
- Total payable (computed)

Typical invoice computations:
- Gross invoice value = Quantity despatched * item price
- Discount = Gross invoice value * discount rate
- Net invoice value = Gross value − discount
- Invoice value = Net value + carriage charges
- VAT = Net invoice value * VAT rate
- Total payable = Invoice value + VAT

Observe that computations are performed progressively, one stage at a time. Refer to p. 147 for the content of the product.

Computer Configuration for Batch Processing

Hardware falls into a number of different categories for specific stages of processing:

1 *Data preparation devices:* Data preparation is normally accomplished by a tape encoder or key-to-disc system consisting of several key stations, supervisor's console, miniprocessor and one or more disc drives.

2 *Computer input: data for processing – input devices:* The choice is dependent upon the nature of the batch processing application. An electricity or gas board, for instance, require optical mark and optical character reading devices whereas a bank requires a magnetic ink character reader/sorter. In general disc drives are used.

3 *Backing storage devices:* A wide selection of backing storage devices are available including fixed and exchangeable disc drives.

Disc backing storage has a wide range of capacities and speed of data transfer which provides a wide base from which to choose. Most installations require two or three disc drives but this is dependent upon the specific installation. Controllers are also required for data transfers between specific devices and the processor.

4 *Output-information devices:* The choice of output device typically relates to the selection of a particular model of printer as batch processing applications have a high volume printout requirement including payrolls and payslips for a payroll application; invoices and statements of account for sales accounting; purchase orders and remittance advices in a purchasing system and so on. It

is necessary to consider the most suitable printing speed, which must be adequate for the amount of printing required. Other aspects such as the width of the carriage require careful assessment.

5 *Control – operator console:* The operator console may be defined as the system interface which enables the operator to input commands to the processor by means of a job control language. The computer displays status and other system messages on the screen to which the operator responds. The console is a visual display unit equipped with a keyboard. The screen displays commands to the computer (input) and displays messages from the computer (output).

6 *Communicating – communications equipment:* If remote job entry is necessary from dispersed offices then modems will be required for data transmission purposes. Leased private telephone lines may be considered necessary to ensure lines are available whenever required. The term *modem* is derived from 'MODulator and DEMmodulator. It is a device connected to terminals in a communication system for converting digital signals received from a terminal to analog signals for transmission by telephone line. This is the process of modulating. When the signals are received at the computer end of the communication line they are converted back from analog to digital by the process of demodulation.

7 *Processing:* The selection of a processor will necessitate an evaluation of the internal memory capacity required and the speed of operation. When discussing the selection of a computer configuration generally, in Chapter 5, the characteristics of processors were outlined. It is also necessary to evaluate the number of communication channels it is capable of servicing and the number of jobs which can be processed concurrently in multi-programming (multi-tasking) mode.

SUMMARY OF KEY POINTS

- Before deciding on the type and size of computer it is necessary to know the processing method to be used.
- Batch processing processes transactions in batches.
- Batch processing is performed progressively – one stage at a time.
- Batch processing is a semi-automatic technique.

SELF-TEST QUESTIONS
1. How is a batch processing application structured?
2. How would you proceed to process invoices and update the sales ledger applying batch processing?
3. Specify the nature of the configuration required for batch processing qualifying your choice of hardware.
4. What factors would you consider in the choice of processor for batch processing?

FURTHER READING

Data processing 1, principles and practice, R. G. Anderson, Macdonald and Evans/Pitman, London, 1987.

Information processing for business studies, A. E. Innes, Pitman, London, 1987.

CHAPTER 12
Processing Techniques: On-line Processing

LEARNING OBJECTIVES

In this chapter you will be introduced to the nature and purpose of on-line processing including the nature of random enquiry systems, microcomputer applications, multi-user and real-time systems. An awareness of the hardware needs for on-line processing including input, storage and output devices and communication equipment is important. You also need to be aware of the application of mixed processing techniques including combined on-line and batch processing.

PURPOSE OF ON-LINE PROCESSING

The important distinction between batch processing and on-line processing is that the latter dispenses with data encoding, as data is input directly by keyboard (*see* Fig. 12.1). With batch processing transactions, data flows into the data processing department from all the relevant departments and is then encoded to magnetic disc. Batch processing is performed by specialist data processing staff whereas on-line processing is carried out by 'users', by means of a terminal connected to a central computer by data transmission lines. While a real-time system is an on-line system it should be remembered that an on-line system is not necessarily a real-time system. On-line processing may relate to transactions which occurred yesterday whereas a real-time system processes transactions as they occur (*see* Real-time systems on page 129). A mainframe computer can support a network of terminals allowing each user a portion of the processor's memory and its available processing time. This is a feature of multi-user systems, which allow each user to process their own specific requirements independently and concurrently (*see* Multi-user systems on page 128). On-line processing includes a number of variations which are referred to in the following sections (*see* Fig. 12.1).

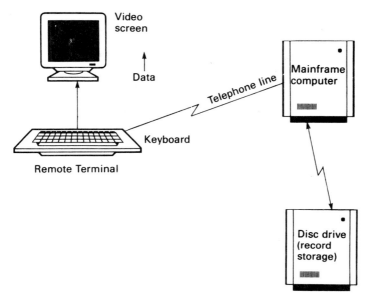

FIG. 12.1 *On-line processing configuration*

RANDOM ENQUIRY AND FILE UPDATING SYSTEMS

For this purpose on-line processing is implemented by means of terminals connected to, and controlled by, the computer. The terminals are connected to the computer by means of communication lines which enable the users to be directly connected to a computer either for random enquiry facilities, such as airline seat reservation systems or on-line enquiry systems such as a bank system to check the status of a customer's account.

MICROCOMPUTER APPLICATIONS

Smaller businesses do not share a central computer for on-line processing but process various menu-driven applications by a business microcomputer. The user is connected to the processor by the system keyboard which is no different in principle to remote terminal operations described above. The distance between the input device – terminal or microcomputer keyboard and the processor (the micro-computer) – can be 10 cm or 10,000 km as there is a world wide network of data transmission facilities available. Business applications processed in this way include stock control, purchase accounting, sales invoicing and accounting and payroll processing etc. The applications normally use menu-driven packages, discussed below.

MULTI-USER AND MULTI-TASKING SYSTEMS

Multi-tasking is the process of running several programs concurrently. It is sometimes referred to as multiprogramming and its operation depends upon the nature of the computer configuration. If the computer has two or more processors then concurrent operation is a reality because two programs can be operated in the same moment of time. If, however, a computer has only one processor it is only capable of processing one program at a time but it switches between operations on different programs at high speed.

Multi-user computer systems allow several users to gain simultaneous access to a central computer through their terminals. This mode of processing shares the cost of operating the computer between the users, but such cost savings must be offset against the cost of the terminal and communication devices – the VDU, keyboard, modem and communication lines, for each user. A powerful centralised computer system is necessary to support and control the concurrent terminal operations. Technically it is only possible to handle one terminal at a time, so high speed switching between terminals by the master control program is necessary to support each terminal without interrupting the jobs being carried out. In a peak processing period the system may create delays due to frequent switching between terminals. This is referred to as 'system degradation'.

Multi-user systems require some form of control to prevent simultaneous access to common files. The technique of *file locking*, which is used for this purpose, restricts access to a file to a single user at any moment in time. This avoids a record on the file being updated by several users simultaneously. When a file is in use, other users of the system are advised. Although effective in some ways, the technique can be very disrupting because the whole of a file is locked even though a user may only be dealing with a small number of records on the file. A remedy to this situation is to apply *record locking*, which only restricts access to the specific record being updated at any one moment. The other users of the system are then able to access other records on the file without restriction. If a record is not being updated, then any number of users can gain access to the record for interrogation, simultaneously (*see* Fig. 12.2).

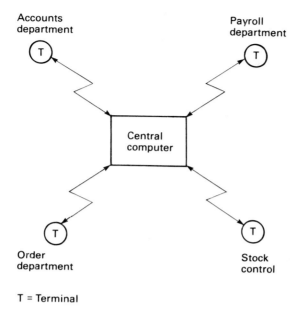

FIG. 12.2 *Multi-user configuration*

REAL-TIME SYSTEMS

Some business systems require critical operations to be controlled as they take place, which means updating the files in real-time, i.e. immediately the event occurs. This applies particularly to applications such as airline seat reservation systems and wholesale food warehouses: both need to be aware of the changing status of stocks. The airline needs to know the seats available at all times on specific flights and the warehouse needs to be aware of the stocks available, or not available, of all commodities, for stock management purposes.

COMPUTER HARDWARE FOR ON-LINE PROCESSING

The specific hardware requirements for on-line processing will depend upon the nature of the applications as discussed above.

The following details indicate the specific needs of particular aspects of on-line processing.

1 *Computer input: data for processing — input devices*

A number of terminals will be required depending upon the number of users connected to the system. With a microcomputer a keyboard will be used to enter data into the system.

2 *Backing storage: storage devices*
A widely dispersed on-line operation will require banks of fixed disc drives and disc controllers to support the file requirements of the various terminals. A microcomputer will require either floppy discs or Winchester fixed disc drives or combinations of both.

3 *Output-information: output devices*
VDU displays information details, menus for selecting processing options, system messages and responses to enquiries.

Printers may be sited at each user location for the purpose of obtaining printed documents and reports. Printer(s) would also be required at the central computer location.

4 *Control: operator console*
Operator console will be required for monitoring the system. The operator needs to be aware of the status of the system, which terminals are on the system, line faults, etc.

5 *Communicating: communications equipment*
If a multi-user system is in use then terminal controllers, modems, multiplexors, front-end processors and private leased communication lines will be required.

6 *Processing: processor*
A powerful processor will be required to support a multi-user environment as it must be capable of polling the lines to allocate time slots to each terminal. It requires a large memory capacity for storing the various user programs as well as the high overhead of storage created by using part of the internal memory capacity for storing the operating system, preventing it being used for application programs. The term 'overhead' in the context of storage capacity relates to the proportion of internal storage which cannot be allocated to application programs because it is required for storing the operating system.

ON-LINE OPERATIONAL CONSIDERATIONS

The proximity of terminals to the computer will determine the nature of the communication lines required for connecting them together. Internal cables may be used for linking terminals up to 1000 m from the central computer.

On-line systems require large capacity fixed disc storage devices to be permanently linked to the processor to take advantage of their direct access capability, as users must have direct access to records on demand. A batch processing system may use exchangeable discs or magnetic tapes, which are removed from the specific devices when a different job is to be processed, and 'exchanged' for other discs or tapes storing the programs and files for the next job.

The function of a front-end processor is to support terminal based operations and remove certain tasks from the mainframe computer. It carries out code conversions, editing, validation, terminal recognition and controls the communication lines. The front-end processor relieves the mainframe of such tasks, enabling it to concentrate on high volume data processing applications.

COMBINED ON-LINE AND BATCH PROCESSING

Order Processing System
Some computer applications are not always processed by a single processing technique; some systems may require processing by a combination of clerical, batch and on-line processing. The previous example outlined a combined clerical and batch processing order processing system. We will now see, using a system flow chart (run chart), the features of a more sophisticated integrated order processing system, consisting of both on-line and batch processing operations. The system is similar to the previous example but the activities of the order clerk are performed by a terminal operator linked to a computer for the on-line entry of orders, checking the credit status of customer and the availability of items ordered. This is shown on the flow chart dealing with this part of the system (*see* Fig. 10.12). On-line processing allows speedy direct access to the relevant customer and product records. The remaining order processing activities are performed by batch processing as shown on the flow chart outlining these operations (batch processing is used because it is an efficient processing method, which allows large volumes of orders to be input and processed without manual intervention). The system also incorporates the printing of a picking list and stock list. Although an integrated order processing system incorporates order acknowledgements, returns from customers, remittances and remittance advices from customers, amendments to product details and customer details, these are not shown on the flow charts, in order to avoid over-complicating the presentation.

Conceptual Model of Order Processing System
When defining the nature of a system for the first time it is good practice to identify the data flows coming from 'sources', flowing to various 'sinks' (destinations). These are shown by the flow lines linking

the circles representing the various entities. The model indicates that a number of entities are external to the order processing system but have a direct link with it, i.e. they are interfaced by means of data flows – such entities are outside the system boundary depicted by a broken line. The entities directly concerned with order processing are the customers, the sales office, the warehouse and the order processing system itself (*see* Fig. 10.1).

Input and Output Documents
The conceptual model of the system may be expanded into more detail by identifying system inputs, files and output documents and reports. These details are shown by a high level flowchart referred to as a block diagram (*see* Fig. 10.10). The details may be summarised as follows:

Input
    a Amendments to product details on the product master file
    b Amendments to customer details on the sales ledger file
    c Order details
    d Returns from customers
    e Remittances and remittance advice notes

Files
    a Sales ledger
    b Product file
    c Shortage file
    d Orders file
    e Invoice file

Output to customer
    a Order rejection advice
    b Order acknowledgement
    c Invalid orders advice
    d Despatch note
    e Invoice
    f Credit note
    g Statement

Output to system
    a Credit status report to credit controller
    b Stock list to stock control
    c Stock shortages to stock control, buying office, production planning
    d Picking list to warehouse

e Daybook to accounts and audit
f Accounts list to accounts

SUMMARY OF KEY POINTS

- On-line processing involves terminals connected to a computer.
- On-line processing is performed by departmental staff not professional computer personnel.
- On-line terminals input data by keyboard dispensing with data preparation (encloding) operations.
- Real-time systems are on-line systems but on-line systems are not necessarily real-time systems.
- On-line processing incorporates multi-user systems.
- On-line systems require large capacity fixed discs permanently linked to a computer.
- Some applications utilise a combination of on-line and batch processing.

SELF-TEST QUESTIONS

1. What are the main distinctions between on-line and batch processing?
2. What systems require random enquiry facilities?
3. What are the main features and benefits of multi-user systems?
4. What type of business activity requires real-time systems?
5. Specify the hardware required for on-line processing.
6. What features must a processor have to support on-line processing?
7. Outline the structure of an order processing system combining both on-line and batch processing.

FURTHER READING

Data processing 1, principles and practice, R. G. Anderson, Macdonald and Evans/Pitman, London, 1987.

Part 6
Computer Applications – 2

CHAPTER 13
Menu-based Information Processing Applications

LEARNING OBJECTIVES

This chapter provides an appreciation of the features of a menu-driven sales order processing system including its features and characteristics, processing operations, various menu displays for selection of options, sales analysis, end of session routine, maintenance of files and output from the system.

USING MENU-DRIVEN APPLICATIONS

Many business applications display a menu for selecting alternative options, as discussed in Chapter 9.

The stages of applying the number selection technique are listed below:

1 Select desired option by keying in relevant number.
2 A message on the screen requests the input of data.
3 The data keyed in is displayed on the screen.
4 The program performs the relevant processing.
5 The results of computations can be displayed on the screen or printed out.

After dealing with a selection from the menu, and further selections are required, it is necessary to return to the menu.

We will now explore a menu-based order processing application followed by an inventory control system in Chapter 14.

MENU-DRIVEN, MICROCOMPUTER-BASED SALES ORDER PROCESSING SYSTEM

System Features and Characteristics

The system to be outlined is menu-driven and is designed for processing sales orders using a microcomputer. The system is based on the BOS order processing software package which provides all the facilities necessary to control sales orders, including all stages of the order cycle – the production of quotations, acknowledgements, picking lists, delivery notes and labels, invoices and credit notes. The software is normally used in conjunction with the inventory control software outlined in Chapter 14. It can be integrated with a sales ledger package for updating customers' accounts with the various order transactions. The integration of sales order processing with the sales ledger and inventory control avoids having to re-enter order data. The system can also be run on a minicomputer with up to 20 screens. The software is designed to be flexible to allow for the varying procedures of different sales offices.

Processing Operations

Input
On receipt of an order the relevant details are input and displayed on the screen. Order details can be amended if necessary. The type of transaction to be dealt with is chosen by selecting the desired option from the main menu, illustrated below:

SALES ORDER PROCESSING

MAIN MENU

```
TRANSACTION ENTRY  ............................................... 1
ORDER PROCESSING  ................................................ 2
ORDER REPORTING  .................................................. 3
END OF SESSION  ..................................................... 4
SALES ANALYSIS REPORTING  ................................. 5
PRODUCT MAINTENANCE  ....................................... 6
SYSTEM MAINTENANCE  .......................................... 7
RESTORE DATA  ........................................................ 8
EXIT  ....................................................................... CR
```

PLEASE SELECT A FUNCTION

If option 1 is selected the screen displays a sub-menu for entering details of transactions, as shown below:

SALES ORDER PROCESSING

TRANSACTION ENTRY

```
ADD ORDERS  ............................................................ 1
ADD INVOICES  ........................................................ 2
```

ADD CREDIT NOTES 3
AMEND TRANSACTION 4
SET SESSION PARAMETERS 5
EXIT .... CR

PLEASE SELECT A FUNCTION

Order processing
Order processing is accomplished by selecting option 2 from the main menu, which displays the order processing sub-menu:

SALES ORDER PROCESSING

ORDER PROCESSING

PROCESS ORDER BY CUSTOMER 1
PROCESS ORDERS BY PRODUCT 2
PROCESS ORDERS BY NUMBER 3
PRINT ACKNOWLEDGEMENTS 4
PRINT QUOTATIONS 5
PRINT PICKING LISTS 6
PRINT DELIVERY NOTES 7
PRINT DELIVERY LABELS 8
CONFIRM ORDERS 9
EXIT .... CR

PLEASE SELECT A FUNCTION

The specific processing required is selected by keying in the option number as shown on the above menu. Credit limit checking occurs when the order is first entered and after each line is added.

Customer details
These are obtained from the sales ledger which includes details of:

- credit limits
- discounting and settlement terms
- invoice and delivery addresses
- nearest warehouse

As each order line is keyed, stock levels are displayed and available stock is allocated to that order. If there is insufficient free stock an alternate product or warehouse can be selected or the order line can be partly or completely back-ordered.

Product Details

Details of the products can be taken automatically from the product file, which contains details of:

- prices
- discounts and VAT
- up to eight list prices may be defined for each product which may be used for different customers, or for different quantities ordered
- up to nine trade discount schemes may be defined; each scheme applies to a set of products and specifies up to nine percentage discounts to be applied to different customers.
- up to nine quantity discount schemes may be defined; each scheme applies to a set of products and specifies up to nine percentage discounts to be applied, depending on order quantity

Flexibility

Built-in flexibility allows for order lines which may be for:

- stocked products
- non-stocked products
- services such as consultancy or labour
- extras such as postage and packing
- percentage extras such as an overall discount
- comments which may be keyed in directly from the screen or taken from the product file.

Output from the System

The order processing sub-menu, see above, also provides for the printing of various documents. The printing of quotations, order acknowledgements and delivery notes can be on special stationery.

Picking List

The picking list is a summary of all orders to be delivered followed by a list of products sorted into warehouse/location order. If warehouse staff detect a stock shortfall not known to the computer this is written by hand on the picking list and the information is keyed into the computer.

Delivery Notes

The order lines show the quantity ordered, quantity delivered and quantity to follow.

MENU-BASED INFORMATION PROCESSING APPLICATIONS 141

Delivery labels
The customer's address can be printed on adhesive label stationery. Additional information such as customer's order reference, delivery date required and delivery instructions may be printed on the labels.

Confirmation of Delivery
Orders can be confirmed and released for invoicing as soon as the delivery notes have been printed. Confirmation of delivery can be deferred until the goods have been delivered.

Order Reporting
Order reporting is a list of orders arranged by customer, product or product range, sales territory, warehouse, delivery date or order number. The orders report can also produce specific reports on any of the above criteria. Order reporting is accomplished by selecting option 3 on the main menu, displaying the following sub-menu:

SALES ORDER PROCESSING

ORDER REPORTING

```
PRINT ORDERS BY CUSTOMER ................................ 1
PRINT ORDERS BY PRODUCT ................................. 2
PRINT ORDERS BY NUMBER .................................. 3
PRINT ORDERS BY PRODUCT GROUP ..................... 4
PRINT ORDERS BY DELIVERY DATE ......................... 5
PRINT ORDERS BY WAREHOUSE ............................. 6
PRINT ORDER BY SALESPERSON ............................. 7
EXIT .................................................................. CR

PLEASE SELECT A FUNCTION
```

Sales Analysis Reporting
The selection of option 5 on the main menu will display a sub-menu screen from which can be selected the required sales analysis report. The menu is as shown below:

SALES ORDER PROCESSING

SALES ANALYSIS REPORTING

```
PRINT CUSTOMER ANALYSIS ..................................... 1
PRINT CUSTOMERS BY SALESPERSON ..................... 2
```

PRINT CUSTOMERS BY TERRITORY 3
PRINT CUSTOMERS BY CLASSIFICATION 4
PRINT PRODUCT ANALYSIS 5
PRINT PRODUCTS BY PRODUCT GROUP 6
PRINT PRODUCT GROUP BY CUSTOMER 7
PRINT PRODUCT GROUP BY SALESPERSON 8
PRINT PRODUCT GROUP BY CLASSIFICATION 10
PRINT CUSTOMERS BY PRODUCT GROUP 11
EXIT .... CR

PLEASE SELECT A FUNCTION

As can be seen by the analysis menu the system provides a great deal of sales information for sales management purposes. It is extremely important to be constantly aware of what products are being sold in what quantities to what customers in what territory by what sales person. Each sales analysis report gives details of amounts invoiced during the current period and the year to date. They include the net sales value, discount percentage, profit percentage, and the units sold for each product.

End of Session and Maintenance Routines

End of Session

At the conclusion of order processing option 4 is selected from the main menu which displays a sub-menu for the end of session options. The screen display is shown below:

SALES ORDER PROCESSING

END OF SESSION

MAKE A SECURITY COPY 1
PRINT CONTROL REPORT 2
PRINT INVOICES 3
PRINT CREDIT NOTES 4
CLOSE SESSION 5
EXIT .... CR

PLEASE SELECT A FUNCTION

Option 1 makes a security copy of all data files and option 2 provides a control report consisting of an audit trail, showing all the new transactions entered into the system and the invoices and credit notes produced, together with any deviations from standard prices or discounts. Another function of the control report is to highlight the percentage of profit made for each order and for each product. Invoices and credit notes are then posted to the sales ledger.

Maintenance of Product File
It is important that the product file is maintained in an up-to-date condition; therefore new products must be added to the file, product details such as prices or discounts must be amended, products no longer marketed must be deleted. File maintenance should be affected before commencing the processing of orders to ensure that the latest information is available from the product file. Product file maintenance is facilitated by selecting option 6 from the main menu. The screen then displays the following sub-menu:

SALES ORDER PROCESSING

PRODUCT MAINTENANCE

```
CREATE PRODUCTS ................................................. 1
AMEND PRODUCTS .................................................. 2
DELETE PRODUCTS ................................................. 3
PRINT PRODUCTS .................................................. 4
REORGANISE PRODUCT FILE ......................... 5
EXIT ............................................................................ CR
```

PLEASE SELECT A FUNCTION

As can be seen on the above menu the appropriate option can be selected according to file maintenance requirements. The product file can also be re-organised by selecting option 5 and the file can be printed out by selecting option 4.

System Maintenance
The order processing system can be maintained by selecting option 7 from the main menu which then displays:

SALES ORDER PROCESSING

SYSTEM MAINTENANCE

```
ALLOCATE DATA FILES .............................................. 1
DISPLAY DATA FILES ................................................ 2
AMEND SYSTEM PARAMETERS ............................. 3
ADD/AMEND REPORT NAMES ............................... 4
```

```
PRINT REPORT NAMES ................................................. 5
SET PASSWORDS ...................................................... 6
EXIT ................................................................... CR
```

PLEASE SELECT A FUNCTION

The relevant maintenance function may now be selected either to change the passwords for added security, option 6, or to amend the names of reports to be produced, option 4, and so on.

SUMMARY OF KEY POINTS

- Many business applications display a menu on a video screen for selecting processing options.
- The stages of selection using the number selection technique include:
    a select option—user keys in option number
    b message requests input—user keys in input data
    c data displayed on screen
    d program performs tasks
    e results displayed or printed

SELF-TEST QUESTIONS
1. Specify the features of a menu-driven order processing system.
2. What options would you expect to find listed on a sales order processing main menu?
3. List typical options shown on a transaction entry menu.
4. What options would you expect to see on an order processing menu (not to be confused with the order processing main menu in question 2).

CHAPTER 14
Menu-driven Inventory Control System

LEARNING OBJECTIVES

The objective of this chapter is similar to that of chapter 13 except to provide an appreciation of the features of a menu-driven inventory control system including its features and characteristics, processing operations, various menu displays for selection of options, end of day routine and output from the system.

STOCK CONTROL OF RAW MATERIALS AND COMPONENT PARTS

Raw materials and other types of materials for use in manufacturing are normally held in the stores until required, when they are issued on the basis of an issue note or issue requisition. An issue reduces the stock available whereas receipts from suppliers or returns from the factory increase the level of stocks. A computerised stock control system automatically tests if the level of stocks has fallen to the point where new supplies are needed, in which case they are printed out on a reorder list.

The purpose of a stock control system is to ensure sufficient stocks are held to satisfy demand on the one hand and to prevent excess stocks on the other. This particularly applies to stocks of consumable food products in a distribution warehouse and stocks of materials and parts for use in the manufacturing processes. Stocks should provide a safety buffer or reservoir to allow for variations in supply and demand. The quantity in stock is kept at the required level by incoming supplies and is drained by outflows to customers or to be used for the manufacturing processes. Stocks often constitute a high proportion of current assets and must be controlled by efficient stock management techniques to ensure they do not exceed an optimum level. To achieve this, stocks are controlled by various parameters, for example, safety or minimum and maximum stock levels, or the level at which stocks should be replenished—the re-order level. To achieve the optimum level of stock—the point when total cost of stock is at a minimum, i.e. the point at which stock holding costs and ordering costs are equal—an economic order quantity is computed.

INTEGRATION OF INVENTORY CONTROL

There are many software packages designed specifically for inventory control systems. The system to be outlined here is based on the BOS—Business Operating Software inventory control package.

Some inventory systems are designed to function on a stand-alone basis but are capable of being interfaced (integrated) with other systems such as an order processing system, the invoicing and sales ledger or the purchase ledger system. Referring back to the order processing system, Fig. 10.12 shows how related activities are integrated to form a composite integrated system.

PROCESSING OPERATIONS IN INVENTORY CONTROL

Input
Input to a typical stock control system and typically includes:

- purchase orders
- despatches to customers (or issues to production)
- receipts from suppliers
- returns to suppliers
- stock reserves for special orders
- stock adjustments for adjusting stock levels as a result of stock taking
- file amendments: additions and deletions

Stock issue and returns are input directly by keyboard or via the invoice and credit note transactions of the related invoicing package or order processing package. Stock ordered and received is input directly to the inventory control system by keyboard. These transactions automatically update the product file.

The action of the various inputs may be summarised as follows:

1 Increases stock quantity
   a receipts from suppliers
   b + stock adjustments
   c returns from customers
2 Decreases stock quantity
   a despatches to customers
   b returns to supplier if relevant
   c − stock adjustments

Processing is commenced by selecting a specific routine from a main menu, as shown below:

INVENTORY CONTROL

MAIN MENU

```
STOCK TRANSACTIONS ............................................. 1
STOCK ENQUIRIES ...................................................... 2
END OF DAY ................................................................ 3
REPORTS ...................................................................... 4
PRODUCT MAINTENANCE ...................................... 5
SYSTEM MAINTENANCE ......................................... 6
EXIT                                                                                   CR
```

PLEASE SELECT A FUNCTION

Stock Transactions

The required routine is selected by keying in the option number as shown above. If option 1 is selected the system displays a sub-menu for processing stock transactions as portrayed below:

INVENTORY CONTROL

STOCK TRANSACTIONS

```
STOCK ORDERED ....................................................... 1
STOCK RECEIVED ..................................................... 2
STOCK ISSUED ........................................................... 3
STOCK RETURNED .................................................. 4
STOCK ALLOCATION ............................................... 5
STOCK COUNT .......................................................... 6
EXIT                                                                                   CR
```

PLEASE SELECT A FUNCTION

The required routine is selected by keying in the relevant option number in accordance with the type of transaction to be dealt with. Option 1 deals with items ordered, from which a stock-on-order report and a re-order report will be produced.

Product File

The product file contains product information including

- product code
- product description
- cost price

- selling price (up to 4)
- stock levels
- VAT and nominal codes
- supplier reference
- standard cost
- last order date
- last sale date
- stock balances – book stock and stock on order
- allocated stock
- stocktaking difference
- statistics
  - cost of sales
  - gross sales value
  - sales discount
  - units sold
  - cost of receipts
  - units received
- nominal code
- quantity discount
- unit designation
- unit weight
- minimum level

The file is updated in accordance with the type of transactions to be posted, which are selected from the stock transaction sub-menu indicated above. Product codes can be predefined in terms of size and alphabetic or numeric content. New products can be added to the file at any time and details of existing products can be inspected and amended. The file can be printed out either in full or for selected product ranges. Product file maintenance is accomplished by selecting option 5 from the main menu. The product maintenance sub-menu is then displayed as follows:

INVENTORY CONTROL

PRODUCT MAINTENANCE

```
PRODUCT FILE UPDATE  .............................................  1
PRODUCT FILE PRINT  ..................................................  2
FILE REORGANISATION  ...........................................  3
STATISTICS MAINTENANCE  ......................................  4
EXIT                                                          CR
```

PLEASE SELECT A FUNCTION

OUTPUT FROM THE INVENTORY CONTROL SYSTEM

Reports

A wide range of reports are provided by the system and report requirements are initiated by selecting option 4 on the main menu, which displays the report sub-menu:

```
              INVENTORY CONTROL

                    REPORTS

    INVENTORY STATUS ................................. 1
    STOCK ON ORDER ................................... 2
    MINIMUM STOCK .................................... 3
    REORDER REPORT ................................... 4
    LEAD TIME EXCEEDED ............................... 5
    SALES ANALYSIS ................................... 6
    COST ANALYSIS .................................... 7
    PRICE LIST ....................................... 8
    EXIT                                             CR

    PLEASE SELECT A FUNCTION
```

Inventory Status Report

Contents:

- product code
- description
- book stock
- stock on order
- allocated stock
- free stock
- re-order level
- unit
- unit cost
- book value at cost

Re-order Report

Contents:

- product code
- description
- re-order level
- supplier reference
- book stock

- stock on order
- lead time
- last order

Product File Print

This report contains details of each product as specified in the product file indicated above. Other reports include those shown on the report menu; these relate to minimum stock, stock on order, lead time exceeded, sales analysis, cost analysis and a price list.

END OF DAY ROUTINE

After completing the processing of stock transactions an 'end of day' routine—option 3, is selected from the main menu, to display the relevant sub-menu:

INVENTORY CONTROL

END OF DAY

```
CREATE SECURITY COPY ............................................. 1
PRINT TRANSACTION JOURNAL ............................ 2
CLEAR JOURNAL ....................................................... 3
EXIT                                                            CR
```

PLEASE SELECT A FUNCTION

The end of day routine provides an audit trail of the most recent stock movements to enable the transactions to be monitored by internal auditors, in order to assess the operational integrity of the system. Security copies of the product file are also created as back up in the event of the master file being corrupted, mislaid or stolen. Option 3—clear journal—allows accumulated transactions to be cleared at any time, ready for the following day's processing.

SELF-TEST QUESTIONS
1. Specify the features of a menu-driven inventory control system.
2. What input would be required to a typical inventory control system?
3. What options would you expect to be listed on an inventory control main menu?

4. What options would you anticipate on the stock transactions menu?
5. State the type of report typically produced by an inventory control system.

Part 7
Computer Applications – 3

CHAPTER 15

Spreadsheets: Concepts and Practice

LEARNING OBJECTIVES

The objectives of this chapter are two-fold. The first is to provide an appreciation of the nature and purpose of spreadsheets together with an idea of their importance in business for the speedy processing of accounting data and the building of models relating to various functional needs including the provision of WHAT IF? facilities for problem solving and other administrative needs. The second is the provision of practical demonstrations of the use of spreadsheets by means of three examples as a basis for practical hands-on experience.

SPREADSHEET DEFINITION

The term spreadsheet is used to describe software which takes the form of a working sheet of 'squared' accountants' analysis paper for recording data electronically, and analysing it.

It is important to plan the layout of the spreadsheet in advance to attain a professional-looking and easy to use appearance. Details displayed will include variables (such as the value of sales and overhead expenses) relationships between variables (such as production costs as a percentage of sales value) and parameters (such as the required annual growth rate of sales). Instead of being a sheet of analysis paper, however, as used by accountants for recording figures relating to a particular problem, the working sheet is a visual display on the computer's monitor. Spreadsheets are widely used for developing financial models for calculating unit costs, projecting profit and loss accounts, and for producing monthly profit projections based on specified growth rates and cost levels. A spreadsheet greatly assists the work of accountants, office managers, corporate planners and administrators as it provides a speedy method of obtaining alternative solutions to a particular type of problem. It allows details to be entered into the computer which are displayed in predesignated row and column locations on the monitor screen. Each piece of data is placed in a particular square or *cell* and formulae can be entered to show how the data in particular cells are related. It is also possible to perform 'what if?' computations. These help managers find out what would happen if sales were increased or decreased by a stated percentage; they can show the effect of variable costs being reduced by a defined amount per unit and the effect on the break-even point of increasing or decreasing fixed costs to different levels according to varying operating circumstances.

OPERATIONAL FEATURES

Once the spreadsheet program is loaded, the screen will display a series of rows and columns. The top of the screen displays a row of letters which name the columns of the worksheet for columnar references. The initial display of column designations may be A–H but the screen can be scrolled (the details moved laterally) to a larger total, perhaps 63 columns, that is; A–Z and AA–BK. A column of numbers is shown down the left of the screen which serve to reference the rows of a worksheet in which details are displayed. Initially rows 1–20 may be displayed but more rows, perhaps 254 or more, can be displayed by vertical scrolling.

There are many different versions of spreadsheet programs available; they may vary slightly in terms of speed, range of facilities and size but generally they are capable of carrying out the following range of activities:

- the content of cells can be blanked.
- a row or column can be deleted.
- a worksheet can be cleared from the screen.
- a command can be cancelled.
- entry of text can be specified as distinct from values or formulas.
- formulas can be entered for specified computations.
- formulas may be examined by displaying them on the screen.
- the display of values may be regained after viewing formulas.
- the worksheet can be saved on disc for future use.
- the worksheet can be loaded into the internal memory from disc for processing.
- either the original spreadsheet framework or one including current values can be printed.
- a report can be displayed on the screen.

- a worksheet can be displayed one page at a time.
- row and column numbers can be deleted and need not be printed.
- the whole of a worksheet need not be printed as it is possible to print specified sections by entering the row and column reference – the range.
- replication of formulas is possible when calculations are similar but when values differ due to amending sales values or variable costs, for instance.
- formatting text is facilitated including aligning text or values to right or left in order to provide a tidy appearance to a report.
- values can be rounded when they have a varying number of digits due to some values having a differing number of decimal places and other values comprising only integers. Unrounded numbers create an untidy appearance.
- the format of a report can be changed, for example, the number of lines per page can be altered and the width in terms of the number of characters.
- rows and columns can be inserted between those which currently exist on the worksheet to provide for those previously omitted.
- rows and columns can be moved.
- formula can be copied into other cells.
- the value in cells can be summed (totalled).
- values contained in a spreadsheet can be converted into bar and pie charts.

A status line indicates the status of the active cell and a prompt line specifies the width of the active cell, the amount of memory left and the cell reference. An entry line displays the information as it is entered by the keyboard.

Entry of Data
Data, text, constants and formulas are entered into specific cells. The row and column which contain the active cell are called the current row and column respectively. The active cell is designated on the screen by the Cursor which is shown as a bar. After data is entered the cursor is automatically moved to an adjacent cell. This becomes the new active cell. It is necessary to indicate whether values, text or formulas are being entered into a cell.

Example 1: Computation of Unit Costs
This example may best be illustrated by outlining the nature of the problem which is essential before attempting a solution.

```
    :  A   : :  B   : :  C   : :  D    : :  E   :
 1:                             Unit cost
 2:
 3:Enter size code in cell A5
 4:
 5: 200
 6:Enter cost per sq metre in    cell A7
 7: 3.00
 8:                              Cost
 9:                               £
10:Material cost                 +A5*A7+2
11:Labour cost                   3
12:Overheads                     4
13:
14:Total cost                    +D10+D11+D12
15:Profit                        +D14*15/100
16:Cost plus profit              +D14+D15
17:VAT                           +D16*15/100
18:Selling price                 +D16+D17
```

FIG. 15.1

The cost accountant of Modart plc, which manufactures fashion garments for the rag trade, uses a personal computer for solving problems which he achieves by writing programs in the BASIC programming language. He considers that the application of spreadsheets will increase his versatility and save time as programming takes a considerable amount of time for a particular application.

The accountant decides to try his hand at applying the spreadsheet technique and selects the computation of unit (garment) costs as the initial problem. The details to be considered for constructing the relevant model are outlined below.

The unit cost of a garment consists of the cost of material used, which is based on the size in square metres, for which a size code is applied, and the cost of a square metre of material. An additional material cost is incurred of £2 per garment for zips, buttons and decorative materials. The labour cost for manufacturing each garment is £3 and the overheads per garment is £4. The cost plus profit is computed by adding 15% profit margin to the above costs. In addition 15% is added for VAT. The spreadsheet is illustrated in Fig. 15.1.

```
    :   A   ::   B   ::   C   ::   D   ::   E   :
 1:                                  Unit cost
 2:
 3:Enter size code in cell A5
 4:
 5: 2.00
 6:Enter cost per sq metre in cell A7
 7: 3.00
 8:                                   Cost
 9:                                    £
10:Material cost                      8.00
11:Labour cost                        3.00
12:Overheads                          4.00
13:
14:Total cost                        15.00
15:Profit                             2.25
16:Cost plus profit                  17.25
17:VAT                                2.59
18:Selling price                     19.84
```

FIG. 15.2

```
    :   A   ::   B   ::   C   ::   D   ::   E   :   F   ::   G   ::   H   :
 1:                    Profit and loss account
 2:                    (for the period ending . . . .)
 3:
 4:                                                       £
 5:Sales                                                20000
 6:
 7:less                                     £
 8:Manufacturing costs                    6000
 9:Administration costs                   3000
10:Selling and distribution costs         3000
11:                                       ____
12:
13:Total cost                                         +F8+F9+F10
14:                                                       ____
15:
16:Gross profit                                        +G5-G13
17:less
18:Interest charges                                     2000
19:                                                       ____
20:
21:Net profit                                          +G16-G18
22:                                                       ____
```

FIG. 15.3

160 BUSINESS SYSTEMS AND INFORMATION TECHNOLOGY

```
     :  A  ::  B  ::  C  ::  D  ::  E  :  F  ::  G  ::  H  :
  1:                 Profit and loss account
  2:                 (for the period ending ....)
  3:
  4:                                              £
  5:Sales                                       20000
  6:
  7:less                                  £
  8:Manufacturing costs                  6000
  9:Administration costs                 3000
 10:Selling and distribution costs       3000
 11:
 12:
 13:Total cost                                  12000
 14:                                            ─────
 15:
 16:Gross profit                                 8000
 17:less
 18:Interest charges                             2000
 19:                                            ─────
 20:
 21:Net profit                                   6000
 22:                                            ─────
```

FIG. 15.4

Construction of the Spreadsheet

The manner of computing unit costs is outlined in Fig. 15.1 which displays the cell references in which text, data and formulae are located. When the formulae are deleted from the screen the final result is shown in Fig. 15.2. If any of the data is changed, such as the size code, then the material cost, total cost, profit, VAT and selling price are automatically recomputed.

Operating the Spreadsheet

The completed spreadsheet should be allocated a filename and saved on disc for future use. The spreadsheet can be printed if required to provide a hard copy for reference purposes. When the spreadsheet is required at a later date it can be loaded from disc into the processor's memory by the load command and entering the filename.

Example 2: Profit and Loss Account

The financial accountant of ABC PLC, manufacturers of electronic components, is interested in using spreadsheets for various tasks. He considers their use would enable him to prepare monthly profit and

```
:   A   ::   B   ::   C   ::   D   ::   E   :   F   ::   G   ::   H   :
1:          Monthly sales, costs and profit/losses for the year 1988
2:                  Sales growth 5% p.m. Costs 50% of sales
3:                                          Total
4:          Sales        Costs         O/H   cost          Profit/loss
5:          £            £             £     £             £
6:Jan       5000         +B6*.5        3000  +D6+E6        +B6-F6
7:Feb       +B6*1.05     +B7*.5        3000  +D7+E7        +B7-F7
8:Mar       +B7*1.05     +B8*.5        3000  +D8+E8        +B8-F8
9:Apl       +B8*1.05     +B9*.5        3000  +D9+E9        +B9-F9
10:May      +B9*1.05     +B10*.5       3000  +D10+E10      +B10-F10
11:Jun      +B10*1.05    +B11*.5       3000  +D11+E11      +B11-F11
12:Jul      +B11*1.05    +B12*.5       3000  +D12+E12      +B12-F12
13:Aug      +B12*1.05    +B13*.5       3000  +D13+E13      +B13-F13
14:Sep      +B13*1.05    +B14*.5       3000  +D14+E14      +B14-F14
15:Oct      +B14*1.05    +B15*.5       3000  +D15+E15      +B15-F15
16:Nov      +B15*1.05    +B16*.05      3000  +D16+E16      +B16-F16
17:Dec      +B16*1.05    +B17*.5       3000  +D17+E17      +B17-F17
18:         ─────        ─────         ──    ─────         ─────
19:         SUM(B6:B17)         SUM(E6:E17)          SUM(G6:G17)
20:
21:                      SUM(D6:D17)   SUM(F6:F17)
22:
23:
```

FIG. 15.5

loss accounts very quickly thereby providing valuable short term information for control of the business. In order to obtain some initial experience the accountant decides to experiment by constructing a simple profit and loss account before embarking on a full-scale profit and loss model. The details to be considered for constructing the relevant model include the sales value for each month from which is deducted the total cost of business operations comprising the sum of manufacturing, administration and selling and distribution costs. The residue, if any, is the gross profit. If the total cost exceeds the value of sales then a loss is incurred. From the gross profit is deducted interest charges incurred on a bank loan or overdraft. The remainder is net profit but if a loss is incurred then the interest charges increase the loss.

Construction of the Spreadsheet

The approach to constructing the profit and loss account is clearly shown in Fig. 15.3 which displays the cell references in which text, data and formulae are located. When the formulae are deleted from the screen the final result is shown in Fig. 15.4. If any of the data is

162 BUSINESS SYSTEMS AND INFORMATION TECHNOLOGY

```
     :  A   ::  B   ::  C   ::  D   ::  E   :  F   ::    G   ::  H   :
     1:       Monthly sales, costs and profit/losses for the year 1988
     2:              Sales growth 5% p.m. Costs 50% of sales
     3:                                          Total
     4:         Sales        Costs    O/H        cost         Profit/loss
     5:          £             £       £          £               £
     6:Jan     5000          2500    3000       5500            -500
     7:Feb     5250          2625    3000       5625            -375
     8:Mar     5513          2756    3000       5756            -244
     9:Apl     5788          2894    3000       5894            -106
    10:May     6078          3039    3000       6039              39
    11:Jun     6381          3191    3000       6191             191
    12:Jul     6700          3350    3000       6350             350
    13:Aug     7036          3518    3000       6518             518
    14:Sep     7387          3694    3000       6694             694
    15:Oct     7757          3878    3000       6878             878
    16:Nov     8144          4076    3000       7072            1072
    17:Dec     8552          4272    3000       7276            1276
    18:                     ─────            ─────            ─────
    19:       79586                         36000                3793
    20:
    21:                     39793                   75793
    22:
    23:
```

FIG. 15.6

changed such as the manufacturing costs, administration costs or selling and distribution costs then the total costs, gross and net profit are automatically recomputed. Similarly, if the sales value is adjusted then the gross and net profit are automatically recomputed.

Operating the Spreadsheet
The completed spreadsheet should be allocated a filename and saved on disc for future use. The spreadsheet can be printed if required to provide a hard copy for reference purposes. When the spreadsheet is required at a later date it can be loaded from disc into the processor's memory by the load command and entering the filename.

Example 3: Sales, Costs and Profit/Loss Projections
The proprietor of Mendquick Ltd, a motor repair business, uses a personal computer for costing the repair jobs undertaken. He has decided to use a speadsheet program to project sales, costs and profit/losses for operations of the following year. He has decided to project

SPREADSHEETS: CONCEPTS AND PRACTICE

	A	B	C	D	E	F	G	H
1:		Monthly sales, costs and profit/losses for the year 1988						
2:		Sales growth 5% p.m. Costs 50% of sales						
3:						Total		
4:		Sales		Costs		O/H	cost	Profit/loss
5:		£		£		£	£	£
6:	Jan	10000		5000		3000	8000	2000
7:	Feb	10500		5250		3000	8250	2250
8:	Mar	11025		5513		3000	8513	2513
9:	Apl	11576		5788		3000	8788	2788
10:	May	12155		6078		3000	9078	3078
11:	Jun	12763		6381		3000	9381	3381
12:	Jul	13401		6700		3000	9700	3700
13:	Aug	14071		7036		3000	10036	4036
14:	Sep	14775		7387		3000	10387	4387
15:	Oct	15513		7757		3000	10757	4757
16:	Nov	16289		8144		3000	11144	5144
17:	Dec	17103		8552		3000	11552	5552
18:		———		———		———	———	———
19:		159171				36000		43586
20:								
21:				79586			115586	
22:								
23:								

FIG. 15.7

the figures on a monthly basis to obtain a short control period. The proprietor forecasts a sales growth rate of 5% for each month for the following year, based on a sales turnover of £5000 for January. He also analyses the relationship between sales turnover and the variable costs of motor repairs and assesses them as 50% of sales turnover. The variable costs include the cost of direct materials and the parts used on the repair jobs; the wages paid to his employees and the cost of direct expenses including paint, welding materials and other consumable supplies. The proprietor then prepares a budget of his fixed overheads of £3000 per month. The overheads include the cost of renting the business premises, local authority rates and cleaning charges; the cost of motor vehicle insurance policy; heat, light and power costs; postage, telephone and stationery costs, etc.

Construction of the Spreadsheet
The approach to constructing the sales, costs and profit and loss projections is outlined in Fig. 15.5 which clearly shows the relevant cell

references and the formulae and data they contain. Note the economical way in which formulae are entered for projecting sales growth and the cost of sales. All that is necessary is to automatically replicate the sales figure in B7 into cells B8 to B17. This is accomplished by the replication command. The formula in D6 is also replicated into cells D7 to D17 in a similar way. Columns F and G are similarly dealt with. The columns are totalled by using the built-in SUM function. The completed spreadsheet after switching from the formulae display mode is shown in Fig. 15.6. If the sales value commenced at £10000 instead of £5000 as shown in Fig. 15.5 and 15.6 then the result would be as in Fig. 15.7. Amending the sales value in the month of January would cause the whole of the spreadsheet to be automatically recomputed.

SUMMARY OF KEY POINTS

- A spreadsheet is software for solving problems by an electronic worksheet.
- It is important to plan the layout of a spreadsheet.
- Spreadsheets are widely used for developing financial models.
- Data is displayed in rows and columns.
- Formulas are used to define the relationship between variables (data items).
- Spreadsheets provide for WHAT IF? situations.

SELF-TEST QUESTIONS
1. What are spreadsheets and for what purpose are they used?
2. How would you commence using a spreadsheet?
3. How would you compile a spreadsheet to compute unit costs?
4. Compile a spreadsheet to produce a simple profit and loss account.
5. Prepare a spreadsheet for sales, costs and profit/loss projections.

CHAPTER 16
Database Concepts

LEARNING OBJECTIVES

The objectives of this chapter are to provide an overall appreciation of the nature, purpose and structure of databases including relational, hierarchical and network structures; the chapter provides a knowledge of the various features of databases including schemas and sub-schemas, device independence, data independence, data dictionary, database management system, fourth-generation language including query language and report generators.

DEFINITION OF A DATABASE

A database may be defined as a file of organized information, or a file of structured data. A typical database would be a record of a business's customers.

The primary purpose of a database is to provide up-to-date information, accurately and quickly. Search techniques enable information which may have been hidden in manual systems to be found easily in electronic systems. For example, a sales manager could find out names of customers in a defined area who purchase a certain quantity of specific products from the company. The information may then be used to establish company policy on quantity discounts.

FUNCTIONAL FILES

The use of a database eliminates traditional functional files which stored common information, which meant that the same data was duplicated in several files. This creates data redundancy and duplicated input; for example, separate functional files often exist for payroll and personnel, each of which stores data relating to employees, such as name, address, employee number, tax code and NI number. If common data is not updated at the same time in each of the separate files the two files would be out of phase and confusion would arise due to conflicting facts being provided from the different files. When data is updated on the database it only needs to be done once: all relevant records will be automatically updated, providing a greater degree of confidence in the data. Databases are accessed indirectly via an internal network or directly by a specific work station or microcomputer with stored database software. A database is available to authorised users; unauthorised users can be locked out or prevented from accessing it by means of passwords.

PUBLIC DATABASES

Public databases provide information relating to a particular topic, e.g. share prices to the general public or to closed user groups. They store and provide data relating to specific subjects, e.g. business, engineering, or science, which is capable of being retrieved by terminals linked to the database via the telephone network. Terminals can also be linked to a database by the Packet Switched Stream (PSS) network which allows users to access distant databases more economically. The data in a public database is supplied by an 'information provider'. A database 'host' is the organisation that owns the computer system and supports the database supplied by the information provider. The database is used by 'information users' who may have to subscribe to the data base.

TYPES OF DATABASE STRUCTURE
Relational databases
A relational database has information stored in two-dimensional tables and relationships between them are defined by each table having one or more common fields. An example of a relational database relates to personnel in a company and the events occurring in their careers, as shown in Fig. 16.1. The relational database in this instance consists of a Personnel table and an Events table. Relationships between the two tables are achieved by the common name field. Each row of a table represents a data record that is stored within the table. Records consist of a set of fields each of which holds one item of information, as shown in Fig. 16.1. The contents of each table is defined by a specification of each field, as shown in Fig. 16.2. A user accesses the database by means of 'forms', examples of which are depicted in Fig. 16.3. The forms include explanatory text, questions and boxes for filling in the answers. The boxes are called 'field windows'. Each field window corresponds to a particular field in an associated table. The first form in Fig. 16.3 is called PER and may be used to enter records into the Personnel table and display records from the Personnel table as shown in Fig. 16.1. Facilities are provided for editing text

DATABASE CONCEPTS 167

Personnel Table

RECORDS \ FIELDS	NAME	INITIALS	BIRTHDATE	DEPT.
1	SMITH, R.A.	RAS	21-OCT-42	4
2	JONES, A.B.	ABJ	19-MAR-51	15
3	BROWN, B.A.	BAB	29-FEB-48	7

Events Table

RECORDS \ FIELDS	NAME	EVENTDATE	EVENT
1	JONES, A.B	1-JUNE-74	JOINED COMPANY
2	BROWN, B.A.	1-JAN-81	JOINED COMPANY
3	JONES, A.B.	15-AUG-79	PROMOTED MANAGER
4	BROWN, B.A.	27-SEP-82	TRANSFER TO STAFF
5	BROWN, B.A.	1-FEB-84	PROMOTED SALES ENG.

FIG. 16.1 *Relational data base example (courtesy D.M. England & Partners Ltd)*

Personnel Table Definition

* * * Table Definition * * *

Table Name . . . . PERSON

Field	Name	Field Type	Total Width	Fractional Width
1	NAME	CHARACTER	20	
2	INITIALS	CHARACTER	3	
3	BIRTHDATE	DATE	9	
4	DEPARTMENT	INTEGER	2	

Events Table Definition

* * * Table Definition * * *
Table Name . . . . EVENTS

Field	Name	Field Type	Total Width	Fractional Width
1	INITIALS	CHARACTER	3	
2	EVENTDATE	DATE	9	
3	EVENT	FREETEXT	0	

FIG. 16.2 *Table definitions (courtesy D.M. England & Partners Ltd)*

within field windows of a form. Characters can be entered from the keyboard at the position of the screen cursor. The cursor may be moved around within a window using the cursor control keys. A query language provides for making enquiries which are expressed as

168 BUSINESS SYSTEMS AND INFORMATION TECHNOLOGY

a set of relationships. English words are used to define commands for performing operations on data records displayed on the screen. Examples of user commands are HELP, ENTER, GET, NEXT, AMEND, QUERY, REPORT.

```
* * *  Personnel Record Form  * * *

Name           [JONES, A.B.     ]        Initials        [ABJ]

Date of Birth         [19-MAR-51]        Department      [4]

Form PER
```

```
* * *  Personnel Events Form * * *

Initials    [ABJ]                        Date   [15-AUG-79]

Event Details

[PROMOTED MANAGER                                          ]
[                                                          ]
[                                                          ]

Form EVE
```

FIG. 16.3 *Examples of forms (courtesy D.M. England & Partners Ltd)*

Hierarchical Databases

A hierarchical structure takes the form of an inverted tree; a trunk with main branches stemming from it and smaller branches stemming from each one. The structure of the hierarchy determines the record types needed and the amount of redundancy (duplicated fields) required. In the case of sales orders, each customer may have several orders relating to the same product, so the product details need to be repeated for each order (*see* Fig. 16.4). The hierarchy defines the route through the database. Access starts at the top and proceeds downwards through the hierarchical structure. Each element may be related to any number of elements at any level below it, but only one element above it.

DATABASE CONCEPTS 169

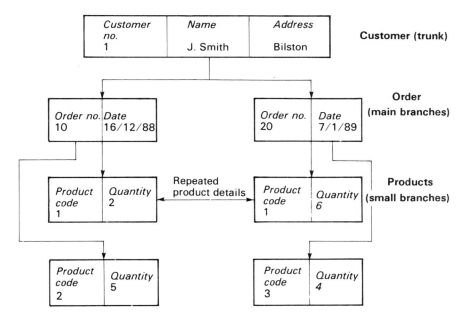

FIG. 16.4 *Hierarchical structure (contrast with network structure)*

Network Databases

A network structure is quite complex because it is representative of the data relationships which businesses contend with as a matter of course. The network is structured on the concept of a set which is a relationship between two record types; for example a product record and a part record. An 'owner' of a set, for example, a product record, can have a number of 'members' in the form of part records (*see* Fig. 16.5). A record type may be a member of several sets, an owner of several sets or a member of one set and owner of another. The network defines the route through the database but the user must know what linkages have been established in the database in order to be aware of the basis for data retrieval. Links between records are established through the use of pointers; a customer record can point to several order records which relate to it. Pointers inform the DBMS where the logical record is located. The next record is indicated by a next pointer (*see* Fig. 16.6). The route to be traversed through a set is to read the 'owner' and then proceed to access 'members' sequentially, eventually returning to the 'owner'. It is not possible to proceed directly from the owner to any particular member because it is necessary to be routed through all the members until the specified member is accessed. This requires the use of next and prior pointers.

Deletion of records is achieved by destroying the pointers which access them. The linkages on either side of the record deleted are maintained by the DBMS. Appending records are also affected by the DBMS which locates the relevant 'set' and locates the record in the most appropriate place. Data integrity is assured by an integrity check utility.

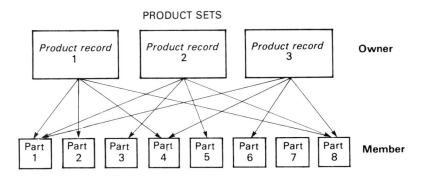

1. The product 1 set consists of members which are part records. The number of part records required for this set are 1, 2, 4, 8.

2. The product 2 set consists of members which are also part records. The number of part records required for this set are 1, 3, 5, 8.

3. The product 3 set consists of members which are also part records. The number of part records required for this set are 1, 4, 6, 8.

FIG. 16.5 *Network structure*

SCHEMAS AND SUB-SCHEMAS

Schemas

A schema embraces the total data in a database and includes details of how records are stored. The schema is stored in the computer and provides the basis for controlling the database. The computer needs to know how to find data in the database which is done by means of location nodes and the information derived from the schema is used by the Device Media Control Language (DMCL).

Sub-schemas

Sub-sets of the schema, known as sub-schemas, provide access to specific data by particular programs. The stock control department, for example, will be unable to access payroll data. The payroll department will, of course, have access to payroll data and have authority to update it. On the other hand, the personnel department will have authority to access payroll data but not to update it. The sub-schema concept provides for efficient control of data which facilitates data

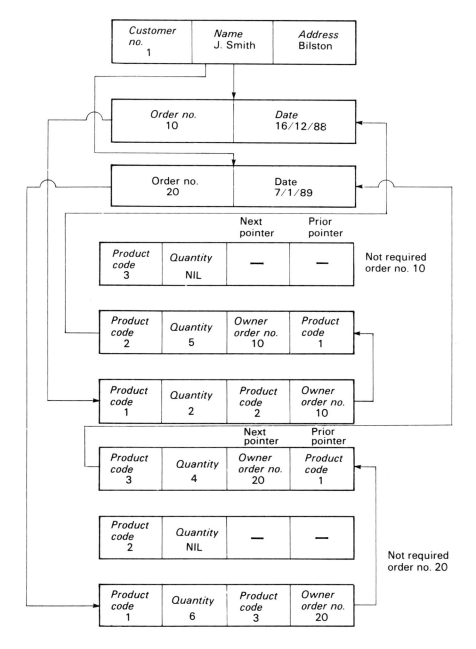

FIG. 16.6 *Route through network illustrating next and prior pointers*

security. In addition, in some implementations, the software necessary to compile schemas is not available to application programmers. This is primarily to maintain privacy as the ability to compile schemas provides the means to bypass privacy checks.

DATA AND DEVICE INDEPENDENCE

Device Independence

The database management system (DBMS) allows data to be independent of any specific physical file. Users of particular applications are still required to define the files to be used in processing but the file has become a 'logical' rather than a 'physical' entity. Users cannot identify their physical file in relation to a particular disc as was the case with separately structured functional files. The reason for this is because the logical data needs of every function are stored in the subschemas. Programs and files are not dependent upon the hardware used to hold the various files. If a file is transferred from one physical disc to another physical disc this can be accomplished without reprogramming. Logical entities are derived from physical entities by means of database software.

Data Independence

Data is stored so as to achieve independence from the programs which use the data. Data structures may change without affecting programs as the structure of the data is held separately and not contained in the programs as it is for traditional file processing. Because of this the size of data fields or the way in which they are structured is of no concern to the user or programmers. It is only necessary to state the fields required to be accessed and the DBMS retrieves them. If any fields are changed it is only necessary to amend the programs that access the particular field. If an additional field is appended only those programs affected by the addition will need recompiling. The operating system refers to a physical file on a specific disc but, because of the facility of data independence, this may be changed without affecting the application software using the data. It is important to appreciate, however, that if a data structure changes this will affect the relationship between records and the way a program navigates around the database will require modification.

DATA DICTIONARY

A data dictionary stores details relating to the data in a database. The dictionary includes: details relating to record structures and their relationships as defined in schemas and sub-schemas; key fields; size of data items; and functional dependencies. The dictionary assists in the development of a database and in reducing the level of redundancy to a necessary minimum. It also avoids duplication of data elements and facilitates easier identification of synonyms, entities having more than one name, and homonyms, entities having the same name as several other entities. Details of data structures may also be incorporated in the dictionary, outlining the way in which data is grouped.

DATABASE MANAGEMENT SYSTEM

A database management system, or DMBS, is software consisting of programs including a Data Description Language (DDL) and a Data Manipulation Language (DML). It allows users to validate, sort, search, update, delete, insert and print records as well as providing facilities for performing calculations, file amendments and maintaining a dictionary. Some systems provide for the printing of standard letters and the merging of text with data, such as names and addresses. Records can be displayed on the screen and browsed through, with amendments made as necessary. File security is also provided for by making copies of disc files and passwords may be used for data protection purposes. Files are re-organised automatically to allow for overflow conditions on disc tracks. Fields may be removed from records and files may be merged or separated according to needs.

Equipment required to run a database
The supplier of any particular database will provide the details of the computer configuration on which the software will run. Database software is designed to be compatible with specified makes and models of computer and a particular operating system.

Database applications
Database applications are wide and varied but typical applications include the preparation of mailing lists and labels. They are also used for major accounting and administrative applications such as the preparation of sales invoices, updating customer accounts, maintenance of personnel records, stock recording and stock management and order processing.

Features of dBASE III +
The dBASE III + software from Ashton Tate, a database management system for personal computers, has a number of features which

will provide you with a greater understanding of the nature of a database management system.

Provision is made for beginners to accomplish day-to-day data management tasks without programming. Specific features to accomplish this include pull-down menus, relational capabilities, context-sensitive help, disc-based and written tutorials.

For more experienced users facilities include: dBASE, a powerful programming facility for database management applications which has an English-like, high level procedural language; and Data Catalog, which organises dBASE III + files. It also includes debugging aids, assembly language calls and environment testing; this lets the user design a system to accommodate various system environments, test the name of the file in use, operate system environment variables, names and numbers of function keys and so on. Routines can be included to be executed when a dBASE III + error occurs or the ESC key is pressed. This feature includes returning the code number of an error or returning the message string of an error. The system also provides for code encryption and linking, providing job protection by condensing source code which prevents unauthorised use and protects against tampering. Command modules are condensed and consolidated into one linked file to save disc space and create a more efficient file.

Other features include report and label generation without programming; applications generator for creating complete applications without programming; screen painter for creating custom screens without programming; built-in networking capability enabling each dBASE III + user to be connected to a local area network, and file access and data protection with file locking and unlocking, and record locking and unlocking facilities. Password protection is provided at eight levels which can be defined for groups, users, files and fields. There are four forms of access at each level – update, extend, read and delete.

The software can handle up to 1 billion records per file, 128 fields per record and 4000 characters per record. It can handle both structured fields, such as numbers and dates, and unstructured fields, such as memos and notes. Data fields can be added, deleted or changed with ease and ten database files can be in use simultaneously. The Assistant screen helps the user by means of a menu bar at the top of the screen showing the main options, including Set up, Create, Update, Position, Retrieve, Organize, Modify and Tools. When a menu item is selected a pull-down menu appears showing further options for that item; for example, if Create is selected this menu will appear:

```
DATABASE FILE
Database file
Format
View
Query
Report
Label
```

A navigation line provides instructions on moving around the screen and selecting an operation. A message line describes the current operation, selected from the pull-down menu.

FOURTH-GENERATION LANGUAGE (4GL)

Query Language

Most database management systems are integrated with a fourth generation query language, a database user language that provides facilities for creating, retrieving, updating, appending, deleting or amending data. A personnel executive may wish to know the numbers of certain employees, and their ages and wages for administrative reasons. Such requirements are formed into a question and the system performs the necessary computations, retrieves the details and presents them to the user.

Refer to p. 189. 'Creating and processing personnel records'; a number of examples of using a query language are provided. Refer to Chapter 9 for further details.

Report Generators

Report generators are an extension of a query language providing facilities for formatting information into business reports, allowing users to define their own formats including rows, number of lines and page numbering. They also produce sub-totals, grand totals and provide for page headers and footers, etc.

Chapter 17 provides a practical demonstration prepared and executed by the author using dBASE II software, similar to dBASE III software but with added enhancements. If you have access to a computer which runs dBASE II/III then you may wish to follow through each stage of the demonstration using the structured details provided in the following chapter.

SUMMARY OF KEY POINTS

- A database is a structured file of data.
- Primary purpose of a database is the provision of data in the required format on demand.
- Search techniques enable valuable information to be found quickly.
- Databases eliminate functional files.
- Several types of database structure exist including relational, hierarchical and network.
- All relevant records in a database are updated with each unit of data affecting them.
- Data is input once only.

SELF-TEST QUESTIONS

1. How would you define the term database?
2. Why do databases eliminate traditional functional files?
3. Outline the features of relational, hierarchical and network database structures.
4. Define the terms schema and sub-schema.
5. A DBMS allows data to be independent of physical files. Discuss this statement.
6. How is data independence achieved?
7. What is the nature and purpose of a data dictionary?
8. What is a DBMS?
9. For what type of application may a database be used?
10. State the features of database software with which you are familiar.
11. What is the purpose of a fourth generation query language?

CHAPTER 17
Database Practice

LEARNING OBJECTIVES

This chapter will help you appreciate how to use a database for processing data to provide specific information. This is accomplished by the provision of two demonstrations relating to asset and personnel records which may be used as a basis for practical hands-on experience.

dBASE II DEMONSTRATION 1: CREATING AND PROCESSING ASSET RECORDS

The demonstration revolves around the creation of a simple set of asset records containing details of the machines used in a factory. The details are minimised for this purpose and each record consists of only four fields: the record number, the type of machine, its cost and location.

The details will demonstrate a number of useful database functions as a basis for understanding just how flexible and powerful a database is. The functions to be outlined include:

- file creation
- input of data to each record
- listing all the records on the file
- listing specific fields of each record
- sum the cost of all machines on the file
- list assets with a cost greater than or less than a stated value
- addition of new records-append
- indexing on specified fields
- finding a record containing a specific attribute
- displaying a specified record
- deleting a specified record
- using a command file
- editing records

Setting up the System
Switch on the computer and when the command prompt is displayed on the screen insert the dBASE II disc in the A drive. Type dBASE

which will transfer the database software to the internal memory of the computer. A copyright message will then be displayed on the screen followed by a command prompt—this is a dot(.).

File creation

It is necessary to decide on the name of the file to be created; in this case it is called ASSETS. The file is then created by the following procedure:

    .CREATE

The system then displays:

    ENTER FILENAME;

At this point it is necessary to enter the filename by spelling it out on the keyboard. The filename should not exceed eight characters and should commence with an alphabetic character and may include digits but no special symbols or spaces. At this point the screen displays:

    ENTER FILENAME: ASSETS

Alternatively, the entry could have been made more directly by means of the following entry:

    .CREATE ASSETS

The next step is to specify the structure of the asset records and for this purpose the system prompts the user by displaying the following details:

    Enter record structure as follows:

    Field Name, Type, Width, Decimal places
    001

A field name may be up to ten characters and may contain digits and colons but no spaces. The fields are of three types:

1. Character = C
   These are for text fields such as descriptions or names
2. Numeric = N
   A number field consists of numbers which may be subjected to arithmetical operations
3. Logical = L
   To be discussed

The width of a field is expressed as the number of characters it can contain which may vary from 1 to 254. The total number of characters per record in this case is restricted to 1000.

If decimal places are required then an extra space must be provided for the decimal point.

The asset records are structured on the following basis:

> Field 1 Name = machine = type of machine
> Type = C = characters to describe the name of the machine
> Width = 20 to allow for long machine names
>
> Field 2 Name = Cost = purchase price of the machine
> Type = N = cost expressed in pounds (£)
> Width = 4 to allow a cost up to 9999 (£)
> No decimal places
>
> Field 3 Name = Location = the departmental location in the factory where the machine is sited
> Type = N = numeric as departments are identified by departmental code
> Width 3 = to allow department numbers up to 999

A record structure is entered as follows:

> Field Name, Type, Width, Decimal places
> 001 MACHINE,C,20
> 002 COST,N,4
> 003 LOCATION,N,3

Input of data to each record

The system then prompts:

> Input data now?

The user responds by typing Y for YES. The screen then displays an outline of the record with boxes for entering data for each field. Each box is representative of the character size of each field.

> RECORD £ 00001
> MACHINE   : 20   :
> COST   : 4 :
> LOCATION   : 3 :

The numbers between the (:) relates to the width of the field in terms of the number of characters.

The first record would be entered as follows:

```
RECORD £ 00001
MACHINE  : CAPSTAN     :
COST     : 1000:
LOCATION : 3 :
```

The entry of a record is terminated by depressing the enter key twice.
The second record would be entered in a similar way viz:

```
RECORD £ 00002
MACHINE  : DRILLER     :
COST     : 500 :
LOCATION : 2 :
```

The third record would also be similarly entered:

```
RECORD £ 00003
MACHINE  : LATHE       :
COST     : 5000 :
LOCATION : 3 :
```

Listing Record Contents

Having set up the database asset records it will be necessary to refer to them from time to time during the course of business and the following details indicate how all records or specified fields within the records could be listed.

1 List all the fields of each record

.LIST

The screen then displays a summary of all the records as follows:

```
00001  CAPSTAN   1000         1
00002  DRILLER    500         2
00003  LATHE     5000         3
```

2 If the content of a specific field is required to be listed the user need only specify the name of the field, e.g. if the type of machine is required this procedure is followed:

.LIST MACHINE

The screen then displays:

```
00001  CAPSTAN
00002  DRILLER
00003  LATHE
```

DATABASE PRACTICE 181

3 Similarly, if the COST of each machine is required then this can be obtained as follows:

.LIST COST

The screen then displays:

```
00001    1000
00002     500
00003   50000
```

4 If it is necessary to know the total value of all the assets, i.e. the machines, then this could be obtained as follows:

.SUM COST

The screen then displays:

6500

5 If a list of machine locations is required then the departmental number of each machine can be listed using the following command:

```
.LIST LOCATION
00001           1
00002           2
00003           3
```

6 If a list of machines and their location is required the following command is necessary:

.LIST MACHINE, LOCATION

The screen then displays:

```
00001   CAPSTAN     1
00002   DRILLER     2
00003   LATHE       3
```

Listing Records with Specific Attributes

1 It is useful to be able to select specific records with a particular attribute from the file. For example, if it is necessary to know which machines have a cost greater than £1000. This information may be obtained by the following command:

.LIST FOR COST > 1000

The relevant record is displayed as follows:

```
00003      LATHE                    5000  3
```

2 A further example:

.LIST FOR COST > 500

The screen displays the two machines which conform to this requirement:

```
00001      CAPSTAN                  1000  1
0002       LATHE                    5000  3
```

3 Another example:

.LIST FOR COST < 1000

This applies to only one machine which is displayed on the screen:

```
00002      DRILLER                  500   2
```

Adding New Records to the Database

To add more records to a file after the initial file has been created the user needs to indicate to the system the file to which records are to be added:

.USE ASSETS

.APPEND

The screen then displays the next record number and an outline of the record structure as it stands. The fields of the new record are entered via the keyboard.

```
RECORD £ 00004
MACHINE  : SHAPER      :
COST     : 300:
LOCATION : 3 :

RECORD £ 00005
MACHINE  : PROFILER    :
COST     : 8500:
LOCATION : 2 :
```

In order to list the previous records in the database and those which have been added, type after the command .LIST and the screen will display all the fields of each record.

Indexing a File

The records in a database are indexed on the field name, referred to as the *key*, according to the attribute required to be listed in ascending order or alphabetically. Indexing a file gives the same effect as if the file had been sorted but the sequence of the records is not physically changed. Indexing creates an index file containing pointers to the records stored in the database file. The index file is stored on disc with an extension .NDX (abbreviation for index). When the original database file is to be listed in a specified order then it is loaded together with the index file and when listed dBASE 11 reads the file in the order in which the keys appear in the index file, giving the effect of a sorted file. Searching an indexed file can be accomplished much faster than searching a sorted file. An index key cannot be more than 100 characters in length. A file may be indexed on more than one key—the first field name is called the *primary key*, the second, the *secondary key* and the third field name the *tertiary key*.

.USE ASSETS
.INDEX ON MACHINE TO SMACHINE

Effectively this routine sorts the records by machine name alphabetically. The system then responds by displaying a message:

00005 RECORDS INDEXED

The indexed file may now be used for listing the database in alphabetical order of machine name, as follows:

.USE ASSETS INDEX SMACHINE
.LIST MACHINE, COST

The system then displays:

```
00001  CAPSTAN    1000
00002  DRILLER     500
00003  LATHE     50000
00005  PROFILER   8500
00004  SHAPER      300
```

The original record numbers remain unchanged but now appear to be out of order. This is because the records have been listed alphabetically by machine name. Alternatively the file may be indexed on the key COST.

.USE ASSETS
.INDEX ON COST TO COST 1

The system then responds by displaying the message:

00005 records indexed

    .USE ASSETS INDEX COST 1
    .LIST MACHINE, COST

The system then displays:

00004	SHAPER	300
00002	DRILLER	500
00001	CAPSTAN	1000
00003	LATHE	5000
00005	PROFILER	8500

Finding a Specific Record
To find a specific record containing a specified attribute such as a particular machine in the asset database file then the procedure is as outlined below.

To find the specific record with a machine attribute PROFILER it is necessary to enter:

    .USE ASSETS
    .INDEX ON MACHINE TO SMACHINE
    00005 RECORDS INDEXED
    .FIND PROFILER
    .DISPLAY

The system then responds by displaying:

    00005 PROFILER   8500   2

If a record having the attribute DRILLER is required to be accessed it is necessary to enter:

    . FIND DRILLER
    . DISPLAY

The system then responds by displaying:

    00002 DRILLER   500   2

To obtain a particular attribute of a specified record it is necessary to enter:

    LIST COST, MACHINE, FOR MACHINE ="PROFILER"

The system then displays:

    00005 8500 PROFILER

Deleting a Record

It is often necessary to delete a record from a file when it no longer serves a useful purpose. The relevant record is marked for deletion as follows:

.DELETE RECORD 5
00001 DELETIONS(S)

The system then marks record 00005 with an asterisk (*) which can be observed by entering:

.LIST

The list shows an * to the right of record 00005

00005 * PROFILER   8500   2

This procedure ensures that the record is excluded from arithmetic commands such as SUM but will be included if COUNT is used. If a file is copied by means of the COPY command the records marked with an asterisk are excluded when the file is copied.

To remove records from a file it is then necessary to use the command PACK which rewrites the file omitting records which have been marked for deletion.

The system then responds:

PACK COMPLETE, 00004 RECORDS COPIED

In order to check that this has been accomplished type:

.LIST

It will be found that record 00005 will not be listed. Use the command APPEND to reinstate the record.

Reinstating a Record

The system has a facility for reinstating records which have been marked but not PACKed. To reinstate record 00005 the following command is required:

.RECALL RECORD 5

To which the system responds:

00001 Recall(s)

Deleting a Group of Records

A group of records can be deleted by the command:

. DELETE NEXT 4

To which the system responds:

00004 Deletion(s)

Records which accord to stated parameters may be marked as follows:

DELETE ALL FOR COST < 500

In respect of the assets file this would cause record 00004 to be deleted and the system would display:

00001 Deletion(s)

COMMAND FILE

The previous demonstration illustrated the way in which the database may be used in direct mode. The database may also be used in programming mode. A Command File containing relevant instructions to accomplish a specified task is prepared. The file is stored on disc and is loaded into the computer's memory when it is to be run. To set up a command file type in MODIFY COMMAND together with a file name into which the commands are stored. With regard to the assets file we may develop a command file to list the fields of the asset records in a specified order. The screen will be cleared and a line in reverse video (a wide band across the screen) will appear into which a command may be entered. The command file is entered one line at a time as follows:

MODIFY COMMAND PROG1	Filename (program name)
USE ASSETS	The file to be processed
LIST COST, MACHINE, LOCATION	The sequence of the fields
SUM COST	The total value of all assets
COUNT	The number of asset records

When the last command line has been entered press the control key and W which will terminate the entry phase and the command file is saved on disc in a file named PROG1. PRG.

To run the command file type:

DO PROG1

The system then displays the field sequence as stipulated in the command file for each of the asset records as follows:

```
00001   1000   CAPSTAN 1
00002    500   DRILLER  2
00003   5000   LATHE    3
00004    300   SHAPER   3
00005   8500   PROFILER 3
```

15300 (sum)
count= 00005

The command file can be modified in line 3 by entering MODIFY COMMAND PROG1 which will cause the command file to be displayed. The third line may be deleted by pressing the control key and Y.

The revised command line may then be entered, e.g. LIST MACHINE, LOCATION. To execute the revised command file enter:

DO PROG1

The system will then display:

```
00001  CAPSTAN 1
00002  DRILLER  2
00003  LATHE    3
00004  SHAPER   3
00005  PROFILER 3
```

DEMONSTRATION 2: CREATING AND PROCESSING PERSONNEL RECORDS

This demonstration creates a set of personnel records consisting of employee name, department, job and weekly wage. Initially the demonstration commences with the records of four personnel but further records can be appended. Personnel are being given a wage increase so records need to be updated to provide for this. An additional field is to be added to record the age of each employee.

The routine for this demonstration is similar to that relating to the previous assets one; it is designed to be used by students either as an assignment or as a revision aid while performing the various routines on a computer.

File Creation

Before creating the file it is necessary to decide on the filename, which in this case will be called PERSONNEL.

Type in:

.CREATE PERSONNEL

The structure of the personnel records must now be specified:

Field 1 Name = name of employee (it is important to enter surname first followed by initials to facilitate indexing)
Type = C = alphabetic characters
Width = 20 to allow for long names

Field 2 Department = place of work of personnel
Type = N = numeric for departmental numbers
Width = 3 to allow for departmental numbers up to 999

Field 3 Job = title to describe type of work
Type = C = alphabetic characters
Width = 20 to allow for long job titles

Field 4 Wage = weekly wage
Type = N = numeric characters
Width = 3 integers only

The system prompts the user by displaying:

enter record structure as follows:
Field Name, Type, Width, Decimal places
001 NAME,C,20
002 DEPARTMENT,N,3
003 JOB,C,20
004 WAGE,N,3

Note: No decimal places are used in this demonstration.

The system then prompts:

Input data now?

It is necessary to type in Y for YES and an outline of each record with boxes for entering each field is displayed sequentially. The width of each box is representative of the character size of each field.

```
RECORD £ 00001
NAME            :              20            :
DEPARTMENT  :3  :
JOB             :              20            :
WAGE            :3  :
```

The first record would be entered as follows:

```
RECORD £ 00001
NAME            :Andrews B C    :
DEPARTMENT      :1  :
JOB             :Toolsetter     :
WAGE            :100 :
```

The second record would be entered as follows:

```
RECORD £ 00002
NAME            :Belcher C R    :
DEPARTMENT      :1  :
JOB             :Operator       :
WAGE            :70  :
```

The third record would be entered as follows:

```
RECORD £ 00003
NAME            :Hemmings D W   :
DEPARTMENT      :2  :
JOB             :Toolsetter     :
WAGE            :90  :
```

The fourth record would be entered as follows:

```
RECORD £ 00004
NAME            :Smith AB       :
DEPARTMENT      :3  :
JOB             :Operator       :
WAGE            :60  :
```

File Copying

It may sometimes be necessary to copy a file to retain the original structure of the initial file. A copy may also be required for amending the original structure. In this demonstration, a copy is to be made of the original file and used for amending with wage increases *see*, 'File updating'.

The procedure is as follows:

```
.USE PERSONNEL
.COPY TO PERSREV
```

The system responds by displaying:

```
00004 records copied
```

File Updating

It is proposed to increase the wages of each employee by 10%. The procedures to accomplish this routine are as follows:

```
.USE PERSREV
.REPLACE ALL WAGE WITH WAGE + WAGE/10
```

This is interpreted as—replace the value stored in the wage field of each record by a value which is the sum of the existing wage value + 10% of the existing wage value.

The system responds by displaying:

00004 replacement(s)

It will be observed that all wages have been increased by 10%. It is possible, however, to update any individual record with any specified wage increase by stipulating the record number in the following way:

```
.USE PERSREV
.GOTO 00001 (or 00002 or 00003, etc.)
.REPLACE WAGE WITH WAGE + WAGE/20
```

This provides a 5% wage increase to Andrews—record number 1.

Adding New Records

As additional personnel are employed they need to be added to the personnel file. Records are appended in the following way:

```
.USE PERSREV (OR PERSONNEL—whichever is relevant)
.APPEND
```

The screen then displays the next record number and an outline of the record structure. The fields of the new record are appended (added) in the normal way.

Deleting a Record

When personnel leave a business it is necessary to remove them from the personnel file. This is accomplished in the following way:

```
.DELETE RECORD 4
```

To which the system responds:

00001 deletion(s)

The system marks the record with an asterisk(*) which can be observed by listing the file.

```
.LIST
```

DATABASE PRACTICE 191

The list shows an * to the right of the record number:

    00004 Smith A B 3   Operator   66

Several records can be deleted by a global command of the form:

    .USE PERSREV
    .DELETE NEXT 3

The system responds:

    00003 deletion(s)

To remove the records from the file it is necessary to use the PACK command which rewrites the file omitting records which have been marked for deletion.

    .PACK

The system displays a message:

    PACK COMPLETE, X RECORDS COPIED

Reinstating a Record

Records which have been marked for deletion can be reinstated providing they have not been PACKed as follows:

    .RECALL RECORD 1

The system responds by the message:

    .00001 recall(s)

Adding a New Field to a Record

If it is necessary to add a new field to a record it modifies the original structure and a command is required to effect the modification, outlined below. It is assumed that a field for Age is to be added to each personnel record and for this purpose it is usual to copy the records to a temporary file. The original file PERSONNEL or PERSREV may be used. The latest file is named PERSREV after updating records with a wage increase and this is the one which should be used in this instance. The required commands are:

    .USE PERSREV
    .COPY STRUCTURE TO TEMP
    .USE TEMP
    .MODIFY STRUCTURE

The system then displays the message:

> Modify erases all records . . . . proceed? (y/n)

If the response is Y the screen is cleared and the file structure is displayed in reverse video. It is now possible to amend the structure by adding the required field. Fields may be added, deleted, decreased or increased in length. If a field is to be inserted between two existing fields—in this instance AGE is to be inserted between JOB and WAGE it is achieved by placing the cursor over WAGE and pressing the control key and the N key. A blank line is provided in which to insert the new field. At this juncture a new structure exists in the file named TEMP but it does not contain any data. The previous data can be transferred to the new file as follows:

.USE TEMP
.APPEND FROM PERSREV

The system responds by displaying:

> x records added.

The new file is renamed with the old filename PERSREV as follows:

.USE TEMP
.COPY TO PERSREV

> x records copied

The TEMP file may now be deleted having served its purpose:

.DELETE FILE TEMP .DBF

The system then states:

> File has been deleted

At this juncture the AGE field is blank. Details may be inserted using either the EDIT or REPLACE command as follows:

.USE PERSREV
.GOTO 00001
.REPLACE AGE WITH 59

This means replace the blank entry in the age field with a specific age value, 59. The procedure is repeated for each employee on the file.

Indexing

Indexing a file on specific fields can serve a good purpose. For example to list names alphabetically:

.USE PERSREV
.INDEX ON NAME TO NAME
.LIST NAME

To list employees in ascending order of age:

.USE PERSREV
.INDEX ON AGE TO AGE
.LIST NAME, AGE

To list employees in ascending order of department:

.USE PERSREV
.INDEX ON DEPARTMENT TO DEPARTMENT
.LIST NAME, DEPARTMENT

To list employees in ascending order of weekly wage:

.USE PERSREV
.INDEX ON WAGE TO WAGE
.LIST NAME, WAGE

Listing Records with Specific Attributes

It is extremely useful to select specific records containing defined attributes as this saves a great deal of time compared with the time required for searching orthodox files. To find the employees whose age is greater than 45 years, for example:

.LIST FOR AGE > 45

Relevant employee records are then displayed.

It may be necessary to search a file for employees whose wages are less than say £80 per week. This can be speedily obtained by:

.LIST FOR WAGE < 80

Finding a Specific Record with a Defined Attribute

To locate a specific record with a defined attribute the following routine may be followed:

.USE PERSREV
.INDEX ON JOB TO JOB

The system responds:

    00004 records indexed
    .FIND TOOLSETTER

This command will result in the display:

    No find.

This is because the data in the job field commences with a capital letter followed by lower case characters. The command must be entered as:

    .FIND Toolsetter
    .DISPLAY

The system then displays only the first record on the file containing the job Toolsetter which is:

    .00001 Andrews B C   1   Toolsetter   59   115

Record three is not displayed even though the job is the same. This problem can be overcome by the following command:

    .LIST NAME, JOB FOR JOB = "Toolsetter"

The system then displays on the screen both records relating to the job toolsetter, i.e.

    00001 Andrews B C Toolsetter
    00003 Hemmings D W Toolsetter

In a similar way the names of personnel in the same department can be displayed by the command:

    .LIST NAME, DEPARTMENT FOR DEPARTMENT = 1

In this instance the system causes to be displayed the following:

    00004 Brewer A C D C   1
    00002 Belcher C R   1
    00001 Andrews B C   1

Display

The concept of the current record is important when using dBASE 11 as it keeps track of the record it is currently working with by means of an electronic pointer. The pointer, unlike the cursor displayed on the screen, is invisible. The pointer moves forward as database records are read in the memory. When a file is first accessed by the USE command the pointer is located at the first record. The pointer may be advanced using the SKIP command:

    .SKIP 4

It is possible to SKIP backwards by the command:

    .SKIP-4

The pointer may be located at the first record by the command:

    .GO TOP

The pointer can also be located at the last record by the command:

    .GO BOTTOM

The command .DISPLAY ALL causes all the records in a file to be displayed – the same affect is achieved by the LIST command.

A number of examples now follow demonstrating some uses of the DISPLAY command.

    .INDEX ON NAME TO NAME
    .GO TOP
    .DISPLAY NEXT 1

These commands cause record 1 to be displayed.

    .DISPLAY NEXT 2

Displays records 1 and 2

    .DISPLAY NEXT 3

Displays records 2,4 and 5

    .GO TOP
    .DISPLAY NEXT 5

Displays all records

    .GO BOTTOM
    .DISPLAY NEXT 1

Displays record 5, the last record as the pointer is located at the last record in the file.

    .DISPLAY NEXT 2 or 3 or 4

Displays only the last record because the pointer is located at the end of the file.

COMMAND FILE

To further demonstrate the use of a command file a primary file has been stored on disc with the filename PERSREV. We may wish to set up a command file for computing the total weekly wages for all employees; the number of employees on the payroll; the average weekly wage; employees earning wages greater than, or less than, average. Such statistics are useful for personnel administration.

First type in MODIFY COMMAND PERSREV. A band will appear across the screen—one for each command. The command file may be constructed as shown below:

```
SET PRINT ON
LIST NAME, DEPARTMENT, JOB, WAGE, AGE
SUM WAGE
SUM AGE
COUNT
SUM WAGE TO WAG1
COUNT TO WAG2
?'TOTAL WAGE PER WEEK IS'
??WAG1
?'TOTAL NUMBER OF EMPLOYEES IS'
??WAG2
?'AVERAGE WEEKLY WAGE IS'
??WAG1/WAG2
?'WAGE GREATER THAN AVERAGE IS'
LIST FOR JOB WAGE > WAG1/WAG2
?'WAGE LESS THAN AVERAGE IS'
LIST FOR JOB WAGE < WAG1/WAG2
SUM AGE TO AGE1
?'AVERAGE AGE OF PERSONNEL IS'
??AGE1/WAG2
?'AGE GREATER THAN AVERAGE IS'
LIST FOR NAME AGE > AGE1/WAG2
?'AGE LESS THAN AVERAGE IS'
LIST FOR NAME AGE < AGE1/WAG2
SET PRINT OFF
```

To terminate the construction of the command file press the control key and W. To execute (run) the command file enter:

.DO PERSREV

The result of processing the command file is then output on the

DATABASE PRACTICE 197

printer and the screen.

Notes to Details in the Command File

Commands preceded by a ? and set between speech marks are printed as shown.

A command preceded by ?? prints the details on the same line as the previous command details.

1	Set print on	Sets the printer on for outputting required details
2	List	Lists the records in the file PERSREV
3	Sum wage	Totals the wages of all personnel
4	Sum age	Totals the age of all personnel
5	Count	Provides a total of personnel
6	Sum wage to WAG1	Transfers the total wages to a store WAG1 for use in subsequent processing
7	Count to WAG2	Transfers the number of personnel to a store WAG2 for use in subsequent processing
8	?'Total wage per week is'	Prints total wage per week
9	??WAG1	prints the total wages on the same line as 8
10	?'Total number of employees is'	Prints total numbers of employees
11	??WAG2	Prints the number of personnel on the same line as 10
12	?'Average weekly wage is'	Prints average weekly wage
13	??WAG1/WAG2	Prints the average wage, i.e. Total wages/Number of personnel on same line as 12
14	?'Wage greater than average is'	Prints wage greater than average
15	List for job wage > WAG1/WAG2	Lists the records containing a wage greater than average
16	?'Wage less than average is	Prints wage less than average
17	List for job wage < WAG1/WAG2	Lists the records containing a wage less than average

18	Sum age to AGE 1	Transfers the total age of all personnel to a store AGE 1 for subsequent processing
19	?'Average age of personnel is'	Prints average age of personnel
20	??AGE1/WAG2	Prints the average age of personnel on same line as 19
21	?'Age greater than average is'	Prints age greater than average
22	List for name age > AGE1/WAG2	Lists the records containing age greater than average
23	?'Age less than average is'	Prints age less than average
24	List for name age < AGE1/WAG2	Lists the records containing age less than average
25	Set print off	Switches the printer off

To display all the records within a file the computer can be instructed to repeat a series of instructions following the DOWHILE (condition) statement up to the ENDDO statement as long as the condition immediately following the DOWHILE statement is true. The DOWHILE statement governs the flow of control within a program which executes a series of loops. When reading and displaying records in a database file the DOWHILE statement is used with the EOF (end of file) function.

The database system writes a marker at the end of each file so that the system can detect when the electronic pointer is at the end of the file. When a file is being read each record is tested to check if it is the end of file marker which is the condition controlling the execution of the program.

The following command file demonstrates the use of the above statements.

To create a command file for this purpose the required commands are:

```
.MODIFY COMMAND LOOP
USE PERSREV
SET TALK OFF
DOWHILE .NOT .EOF
DISPLAY
SKIP
ENDDO
?
```

?'THE EOF MARKER HAS BEEN REACHED'
?'THERE ARE NO MORE RECORDS'
?'END OF RUN'

The command file can be executed by the command:

.DO LOOP

The command file then displays the contents of each personnel record on the file as shown below:

```
00001  Andrews B C      1 Toolsetter        59   115
00002  Belcher C R      1 Operator          35    77
00003  Hemmings D W     2 Toolsetter        45    99
00004  Brewer A C D C   1 Maintenance       28    75
00005  Brewer J K       3 Progress clerk    56    85
```

THE EOF MARKER HAS BEEN REACHED
THERE ARE NO MORE RECORDS
END OF RUN

SELF-TEST QUESTIONS
1. Set up a database for creating and processing asset records based on the demonstration provided in the text.
2. Set up a simple file for listing the cost, machine and location for each asset, the total value of all assets and the number of asset records on the file.
3. Set up a database for creating and processing personnel records based on the demonstration provided in the text.
4. Set up a command file for processing personnel records based on the demonstration provided in the text.

CHAPTER 18
Introduction to Knowledge Based Systems

LEARNING OBJECTIVES

This chapter provides an understanding of the branch of artificial intelligence known as knowledge based systems. It is necessary to be aware of the manner of collecting knowledge from an expert by a knowledge engineer. It is also necessary to appreciate the importance of knowledge based systems in the modern business world, and their nature, structure and purpose. It is also important to be aware of the development tools available for the construction of knowledge based systems.

CHARACTERISTICS OF KNOWLEDGE BASED SYSTEMS

Knowledge based systems (KBS) which are sometimes called expert systems may be defined as computerised systems which simulate human knowledge by making deductions from given facts using the rules of logical inference. They belong to that branch of knowledge or information technology relating to artificial intelligence.

Applications
The use of KBS depends on a particular system's sophistication. At present they are used for diagnosing illnesses from symptoms indicated by the patient, for diagnosing faults in complex machines such as computers, and for diagnosing problems in business systems.

Collecting Knowledge
The development of KBS requires a high degree of co-ordination between researchers, sometimes referred to as knowledge engineers, and experts of a defined subject, known as domain experts. The experts are interviewed by researchers to assess ways of collecting and transferring their knowledge into knowledge-based computerised systems. This necessitates an analysis of how experts

analyse a problem. Establishing structure to the volume of details collected from the experts is a major problem as there are many cause and effect relationships, one leading to another in an apparently never ending uncoordinated stream. Interviewers attempt to remedy the lack of structure by carefully planning the questions to be asked during interviews to avoid possible omission of important facts but knowledge does not flow from the mind of the expert in such a structured form. During interviews it is a practical proposition to record facts on a tape recorder for future analysis.

STRUCTURE OF A KBS

The core of a KBS is the *rules* it works to. These rules define the relationship between facts so that if a particular situation exists THEN a particular action must occur. An expert system consists of three primary elements: an inference engine which acts as a rule interpreter; a knowledge base which is the heart of the system containing rules; and a database consisting of facts relating to a particular domain, i.e. subject area. *See* Fig. 18.1.

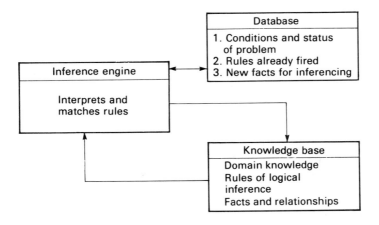

FIG. 18.1 *Outline structure of knowledge-based system*

Inference Engine and Knowledge Base

An inference engine is an element of an expert system which functions in combination with the knowledge base. The knowledge base stores knowledge of a specific subject in the form of facts and relationships. The inference engine questions the user and interprets the rules of relationship.

Inferencing

Inferencing is the process of reaching a solution or decision by reasoning, of drawing a conclusion from given evidence. In effect it simulates the human thinking process; in this way an expert system differs from traditional computer programs which have built-in logic often derived from the details contained in decision tables prepared for the purpose. The system provides for every condition that may occur in a system together with the relevant action in accordance with specified rules. A computer program does not therefore have an inference facility.

Database

An expert system database is an area of working memory which stores initial conditions of the problem to be solved and details of the current status of the problem. It stores known facts and new facts are added from the inference process.

Explanation of Reasoning

It is important to appreciate that a user may not agree with or understand an answer provided by a knowledge based system and in such instances a user will want to know how the system arrived at its conclusion. The system may do this by displaying the rules which formed the basis of the conclusion and the sequence in which they were dealt with from details stored in the database. In this way the user can assess the line of reasoning by going through the rules sequentially assessing the logic inference at each stage of assessment. Some systems incorporate explanatory statements in the rule which may be studied by the user. This is an important facility because it provides confidence in the system which is essential for making decisions based on the conclusions provided.

Amendments

It is, of course, possible to amend rules if they prove to be ambiguous or inaccurate. The integrity of the knowledge base is a function of the accuracy of the knowledge it contains and the degree to which it relates to current circumstances. Some business systems frequently change the control parameters in various systems as policy or circumstances change. The parameters are used, for example, as a basis for granting credit to customers; for determining the level of stocks; for reordering stocks; changes to the value of sales or the distance of deliveries to customers as a basis for making delivery charges and so on. This is the subject of the example provided later in the text.

Adaptive Learning

Knowledge based systems, to differentiate them from decision table processors, must be able to learn from their own experience. During the course of processing, the inference engine (a rule interpreter) will make conclusions which generate new knowledge. (When is a KBS not a KBS? When it is only a decision table processor which cannot generate new knowledge and can only process the built-in knowledge.) Newly generated knowledge is stored in the database and can cause a new rule to be created and stored in the knowledge base (stores rules) which can be applied to future uses of the system. Learning in this context may be inferred to mean the process of teaching the system new knowledge by the addition of new rules or the amendment of existing rules. A powerful KBS will have the built-in ability to learn itself.

RULES

Rules form part of the knowledge base of these systems. They define relationships between facts and may be defined as representations of human reasoning which in combination with an antecedent specify an inference on which to base a specified action. Details are input to the knowledge base in the form of 'production rules', each representing an individual item of knowledge. Rules combine to form a line of reasoning. The conclusion of one rule may become the premise of another and it is this collection of rules that combine to form the knowledge base. Each production rule consists of two parts. The left-hand side contains an IF clause consisting of a premise or condition. The right-hand contains a THEN clause consisting of a conclusion, action or consequence. If the premises in the left-hand part of a rule are true or the condition is met, the right-hand part is also true. The rule is then 'triggered'. When the right-hand side of the rule is implemented it is said to be 'fired'. This process consists of taking a specified action when specific situations are true on the basis of—If A is true AND B is true THEN do a stated action. Production rules are useful for representing all types of knowledge for attaining goals. Every rule has one IF clause and one THEN clause and may also contain an ELSE clause. A clause is similar to a sentence with a subject, a verb and an object that states some fact. Clauses can be linked by the conjunctions AND or OR. For example: IF the value of sales is less than £50 AND the delivery distance is greater than 20 miles THEN charge for delivery ELSE do not charge for delivery. This may be interpreted to infer that if the sales value is greater than £50 do not charge for delivery. The system may require charging for delivery on a different basis using the OR conjunction in the form—IF the value of sales is less than £50 OR the delivery distance is less than 20 miles THEN do not charge for delivery. Existing rules can be modified and new rules added to the knowledge base. Rules are stored in the computer's memory which is where the inference engine interprets them. Most commercial expert systems apply the IF–THEN format. A conclusion is indicated by the THEN part of a rule. This format is also widely applied in computer programming using a language such as BASIC and when solving logical problems by the application of structured English.

DEALING WITH UNCERTAINTY

Knowledge based systems are able to deal with incomplete or uncertain details relating to a problem. When the system displays a question on the screen the user may not have a precise answer or even an answer at all. Knowledge based systems are designed to deal with this situation and will provide a solution even though an input is missing or ambiguous. The system, in such instances, may qualify the answer given based on the available facts. In some instances this aspect can be catered for by the inclusion of rules to deal with the situation when information is not known which will trigger a specific action. Decisions are often made in business in the absence of complete facts so a knowledge based system in such instances copies the real world. Normal programs are structured on an algorithmic basis whereby instructions consist of a series of IF–THEN–ELSE statements as illustrated in the example in this chapter relating to the processing of customers' orders. A knowledge based system in which the rules can be stated algorithmically and uncertainty is not inherent in the problem to be solved— such as the example quoted above—is similar to a decision table processor.

Certainty factors

The degree of certainty of a condition occurring is determined by the domain expert who may assess them from experience or published statistics such as the probability of male smokers dying from cancer below the age of 60, or the number of days in a year that it rained. In other instances the degree of certainty may be assessed by pure 'guestimating'. Certainty or confidence factors are used with the IF and THEN clauses of a rule. The degree of certainty may be based on a scale of 0 to 1 whereby 0 represents no certainty at all, that is 100% uncertainty, and 1 represents 100% certainty. Other intermediate degrees of certainty can be established from the scale. The inference engine decides if a specific rule is to be fired on the basis of its evaluation of the confidence factor which may require to be above a predefined value. In rules consisting of multiple premise clauses connected by AND or OR, each clause has its own confidence factor. This situation requires a composite confidence factor for the rule. For those clauses connected by AND this is accomplished by applying what is referred to as the 'minimum confidence factor' which is demonstrated below. If condition A has a confidence factor (CF) of 0.5 (a 50% probability of occurrence) AND condition B has a CF of 0.8 (an 80% probability of occurrence) THEN C. This may be stated in Structured English as shown in Example 1:

Example 1:   IF A = 0.5
     AND B = 0.8
     THEN C
  The CF = 0.5 (minimum CF)

For those clauses which are connected by OR the composite CF is established by the application of the 'maximum confidence factor' which is demonstrated in example 2.

Example 2:   IF D = 0.5
     OR E = 0.8
     THEN F
  The CF = 0.8 (maximum CF)

The CF of each rule in a reasoning chain will affect the others and the outcome is dependent upon the composite CF which may be stated— if the CF for rule 1 is added to the CF for rule 2 from which is subtracted the product of the CFs for rules 1 and 2. For example:

Rule 1: IF G
    AND H
    THEN I = 0.55

Rule 2: IF I
    THEN J = 0.4

CF = CF(I) + CF(J)   − CF(I) * CF(J)
 = 0.55 + 0.4   − 0.55 * 0.4
 = 0.95   − 0.22 = 0.73

In circumstances when the number of rules in a chain exceeds two it is necessary to apply the CF of two rules and combine this with the CF of a third rule to obtain the CF. This routine continues for all the rules in a chain to compute the CF for the complete chain.

Probability
Many KBS have multiple probability situations to provide for whereby the overall probability of a rule is the product of individual probabilities. In such instances the parts of the antecedent are independent of each other. If a rule has four parts to its antecedents with the probabilities of 0.5, 0.3, 0.2 and 0.1 then the overall probability is P = (0.5) (0.3) (0.2) (0.1) = 0.003 or 3%. There is a need to assess the total probability of a sequence of rules to determine if a specific rule is applicable which is then fired. Alternatively, the combined probability may be used as a basis of determining the most suitable search path. Most conditions and rules are generally dependent upon each other in which case Bayes' theorem can be applied to compute the probability of condition A occurring given that B has already occurred. It is beyond the scope of this book, however, to go into greater depth of probability theory. In any event Bayesian probability is used by many KBS development aids.

Fuzzy Logic
Fuzzy logic is a means of dealing with unreliable or perhaps imprecise data. The method attempts to allocate a value between 0 and 1 to attributes imprecisely defined. An assigned value between 0 and 1 signifies that there is some degree of possibility that an attribute is within a given range. This may apply when attempting to define high or low production volume. What is a high volume and what is a low volume? A measure of the volume of production depends upon the normal achievements of a small business which may be of an entirely different magnitude to that of a large business. The small volume of a large business may be a large volume of a small business. Volume must be specific to particular situations and a high volume must be given a range of values to which that designation applies. A low volume must also be given a different range of values to which that designation applies. The derived values must be accompanied by a relevant probability factor. In such instances a 0 possibility means that volume is not in the range given but a possibility of 1 implies that volume is within the range of values. This approach facilitates the reasoning process but is not so widely used as confidence factors.

MODUS OPERANDI

Backward and Forward Chaining
A KBS can work in either of two ways. By working backwards through supporting evidence to establish the truth of a previously selected conclusion, by applying backward chaining or by forward chaining which commences with appraising the evidence as a basis for selecting a goal emanating from them. Declarative languages such as Prolog and Lisp are used to describe the relationships between data.

Heuristic process
The heuristic process is applied to knowledge in the knowledge base by the process of 'rule of thumb' reasoning when it is impossible to reach a solution by normal logical processes. This can arise because of the large number of possible combinations. This is accomplished by rule-based programming, where rules of logical inference are contained in the knowledge base.

Providing a solution
The provision of a solution to a problem commences in one of two possible ways either by displaying a menu of options from which to choose or by asking questions to which answers are typed in. This triggers off the search process. The inference engine is the rule interpreter and it searches the knowledge base to match the rules with the information stored in the database. Each rule is examined and any actions effected when a rule is fired may change the content of the database updating the status of the problem. New facts often materialise which may be applied in providing a solution to the problem. The system may also make requests for additional information from the user. The database stores a list of rules which have already been inspected and fired and the sequence in which they occurred. The rule sequence can subsequently be provided to the user as a basis of understanding the underlying reasoning which has been applied. The inference engine (rule interpreter) examines the rules in a particular sequence looking for matches to the conditions in the database. As rules are matched with the conditions the rules are fired effecting the specified actions. As rules are fired they are referenced to each other to form an inference chain. When each new rule is examined it is compared with the current status of the solution in the database.

DEVELOPMENT TOOLS

Software for building knowledge based systems

Software is available for building knowledge based systems from software houses specialising in this branch of artificial intelligence. This type of software is known as a shell, generator or builder. A shell provides a basic framework in which data, rules or knowledge can be input and processed. A shell does not contain a knowledge base but provides facilities for their creation for specific subject areas or domains as they are called. Some packages allow rules to be typed in as notes or full sentences and do not require syntax, a rule language or compilation. A dictionary can be used to copy and select rules. Full text and graphic screens can be used to illustrate answers, advice or questions, Logical operators can be used in any combination at any level of the structure. Some software has a menu interface and facilities for linking with other software for mathematical computations or to a natural language processor, for instance. Some software provides for an alphabetic listing of all the rules in the system together with each piece of evidence and text, with cross references. The evidence behind any conclusion is explained as is the reasoning behind any questions, which allows the user to explore or navigate the entire logic of the system. A generator has an editor allowing knowledge to be input in a predetermined rule format and the generator compiles them into the code the system requires for processing. Many shell and generator packages use the IF–THEN rule structure as illustrated in the example which follows, relating to processing customers' orders. Other shells do not require the IF–THEN structure but establish knowledge from a matrix in the form of a decision table. Each column of the matrix represents a rule consisting of the various combinations of conditions which exist in the subject under consideration. Outcomes or decision are listed in the rule columns for each combination of conditions. Regardless of the type of development tool it is necessary to establish all the possible conditions that can arise and for each set of conditions rules are established and the actions or decisions to be taken are determined. The matrix then defines the knowledge in the system.

Languages

The most popular languages for developing KBS are LISP and Prolog which were designed for artificial intelligence applications.

Knowledge based systems have been developed using many different languages including BASIC, Fortran, C, Forth and Pascal. Expert programmers may elect to develop knowledge based systems using these languages but it is often preferable to use expert system shells.

KNOWLEDGE BASED SYSTEM: PROCESSING CUSTOMERS ORDERS

The problem to be outlined for the purpose of demonstrating the characteristics and use of a knowledge based system relates to the processing of customers orders. The action taken is dependent upon the existence of specific conditions according to the rules of logical inference built into the knowledge base.

The decision to accept an order depends on the credit status of the relevant customer from whom the order is received. To establish credit status it is necessary to value the order, add the value to current account balance and compare the total with the credit limit. If the sum of the account balance and the value of the order is equal to, or less than, the credit limit then the order is accepted; otherwise it is rejected.

It is then necessary to establish if the whole of the order, i.e. the full quantity of each item, can be despatched; this depends on whether the quantity in stock is equal to, or greater than, the order quantity. If it is less than the order quantity then it is only possible to despatch a part order. This situation requires shortages to be entered on a back-order report for maintaining a record of outstanding items. In all instances when an item is despatched it is necessary to determine if it should be re-ordered to avoid future shortages. It may have reached the re-order level after the despatch of items therefore; if the quantity in stock is equal to, or less than, the re-order level it should be re-ordered.

It is also necessary to determine if a charge should be made for delivery. Company policy in this respect is based on order value and delivery mileage. If the value of the order is less than £50 and the delivery distance is less than 20 miles then no charge is made for delivery. If, on the other hand, the value of the order is less than £50 and the delivery distance is greater than 20 miles then a charge is made for delivery. In all other instances no charge is made. This implies that if the order value is greater than £50 and the delivery mileage is greater than 20 miles then no charge is made.

The above details are resolved into clauses forming production rules, forming the knowledge base, which are defined in Table 1. Table 1 also states the problems to be resolved. The answers to the questions displayed on the screen are stored in the database providing the initial conditions of the problem. More facts are added from the inference process.

TABLE 1

Problem	Production rule: knowledge base (rule base)	
	a. Left hand side IF clause (premise or condition)	b. Right hand side THEN clause (conclusion, action or consequence)
1. Is credit status satisfactory A. What is the account balance? B. What is the value of the order? C. What is the credit limit?		
	a. IF account balance (A) AND value of order (B) is equal to or less than credit limit (C)	b. THEN (H) accept order ELSE reject order (I)
2. Is there sufficient stock to despatch complete order? D. What is the quantity in stock? E. What is the order quantity?		
	a. IF quantity in stock (D) => order quantity (E)	b. THEN despatch complete order (J)
	a. IF quantity in stock (D) > E	b. THEN despatch part order (K) and place items in short supply on back-order report (L)
3. Should items be reordered? F. What is the re-order level?		
	a. IF the quantity in stock (D) = < re-order level (F)	b. THEN re-order (M)

INTRODUCTION TO KNOWLEDGE BASED SYSTEMS

4. *Is delivery chargeable?*
B. What is the value of the order (see p. 210)?
   a. IF the value of the order (B) is less than £50 OR the distance (G) is less than 20 miles
   b. THEN no charge for delivery (N)

G. What is the delivery mileage?
   a. IF the value of the order (B) is less than £50 AND the delivery distance (G) is greater than 20 miles
   b. THEN charge for delivery (O)

MODUS OPERANDI

We will now analyse the processes after the initial conditions, consisting of answers to questions, have been input to the database. The premises and conditions listed below:

A. Account balance
B. Value of order
C. Credit limit
D. Quantity in stock
E. Order quantity
F. Re-order level
G. Delivery mileage

Inferred conclusions, actions or consequences are derived from the process of forward chaining performed by the inference engine after interpreting and matching rules in the knowledge base with information stored in the database. These are listed below:

H. Accept order
I. Reject order
J. Despatch complete order
K. Depatch part order
L. Place on back-order report
M. Re-order
N. No charge for delivery
O. Charge for delivery

The details contained in Table 2 summarise the details provided in Table 1.

TABLE 2 *Rule base*

1. IF A AND B =< C THEN H ELSE I
2. IF D => E THEN J
3. IF D > E THEN K AND L
4. IF D =< F THEN M
5. IF B < £50 OR G < 20 THEN N
6. IF B < £50 AND G > 20 THEN O

The inference engine selects the first known fact A and begins searching through the rule base looking for a premise or condition in the IF part of the rule which matches it. All the rules are examined sequentially. There is a match in rule 1 but to fire the rule B and C are also required. The inference engine, the rule interpreter, accesses the database to search for B and C which are present and fires rule 1. Inferred clauses specifying the required action H and I are added to the database.

No other rules contain A and the inference engine proceeds to the next rule in sequence which is B. It accesses B from the database and proceeds to search for a match. A match exists in rule 5 but G is also a condition for the rule which the inference engine finds in the database. Rule 5 is fired and N is added to the database. Rule 6 also contains condition B which also requires condition G which already exists in the database. Rule 6 is fired and 0 is inferred which is added to the database.

The inference engine than accesses the condition C from the database and searches the rule base for a matching rule. No match exists.

As no match exists the next condition, D, is selected which is contained in rule 2. Rule 2 also requires E which exists in the database. Rule 2 is fired and J is inferred which is added to the database. Rule 3 also contains condition D but condition E is also required for this rule. Condition E exists in the database. The rule is fired and K and L are inferred and they are added to the database. Rule 4 also contains condition D which also requires conditions F OR K for this rule and the inferencing engine checks the database and finds F and K in the database, M is inferred, the rule is fired and M is added to the database.

The inference engine then selects E from the database and does not find a match in any of the rules. Condition F is then selected and the rules searched for a match which does not exist. The inference engine proceeds to G which also does not exist in the rules and the process is concluded.

INTRODUCTION TO KNOWLEDGE BASED SYSTEMS

SUMMARY OF KEY POINTS

- Knowledge based systems are a branch of artificial intelligence.
- KBS simulate human knowledge by making deductions from given facts.
- Knowledge engineers collect knowledge from domain experts.
- The structure of a KBS includes an inference engine, knowledge base and a database.
- KBS must be able to learn from experience.
- A KBS is able to deal with incomplete knowledge and uncertainty.
- A KBS can apply backward or forward chaining.
- Rules form part of the knowledge base.
- Rules define the relationship between facts.

SELF-TEST QUESTIONS

1. What is a knowledge based system and how are they applied?
2. State how knowledge is collected for forming a KBS.
3. Define the following terms relating to a KBS: inference engine, inferencing, knowledge base and database, forward chaining and backward chaining.
4. What is meant by 'adaptive learning'?
5. What part of a KBS interprets rules?
6. What is stored in a knowledge base?
7. How is uncertainty dealt with in a KBS?
8. What is shell?
9. What languages are most popular for developing KBS?

FURTHER READING

Crash course in artificial intelligence and expert systems, Louis E. Frenzel, Jr, Howard W. Sams, 1987.

CHAPTER 19
Networks

LEARNING OBJECTIVES

Communication networks are vital in the modern business world. It is important to appreciate the usefulness of network resources in providing efficient communications between local offices and between dispersed computers and terminals by the various types of network. Networks provide the means for the speedy transfer of data between locations and the provision of speedy responses to enquiries.

LOCAL AREA NETWORK

Nature and Purpose

A local area network (LAN) is designed to serve a local establishment such as a factory and its administrative offices, and is a speedy and effective means of communication between the various sections of the business. A LAN consists of a number of interconnected microcomputers, terminals, printers and work stations forming a network providing *distributed processing* facilities. Distributed processing provides computing facilities in the various locations of a business such as the sales office, accounts department, the warehouse and production control. This is in contrast to all information processing being done at one installation, known as *centralised processing*. In such instances all data is channelled to the central computer from all the departments. Networks have different topologies, protocols and methods of data transmission; the type of cable used varies and may be twisted-pair, coaxial or fibre-optic cable.

Shared Resources and Facilities

LANs share expensive resources, e.g. high speed printers, and high capacity discs which are accessible to all authorised users of the network.

Various facilities are required to enable networks to function. They include a communication server for linking network users to communication devices by telephone line connections; a print server providing each network user with high speed printing facilities; and a file server facilitating the storage of software and information files which can be retrieved and updated as necessary. LANs can be either broadband or baseband. *Broadband* networks have a number of channels multiplexed together, one of which serves as a high speed data channel and one is available for other purposes such as video. A *baseband* channel only provides for data transmission in one direction at a time. It uses lower cost cable than broadband because of the lower band width required for a single channel.

Gateways
Two-way communication is possible between the various computers in the network for transferring data or messages electronically by electronic mail. The speed of transmission can be up to 12,000,000 bits per second. Modems can link LANs to the public telephone system and gateways to other networks providing facilities for teleshopping and airline seat reservations.

NETWORK TOPOLOGY

Ring Network
A ring network is structured as a continuous ring of *nodes*, or devices, each linked to the next in the ring (*see* Fig. 19.1). Each device has a unique identification address. Messages are passed from one node to the next until the node for which the message is intended, as indicated by the address, is reached. These networks are sometimes called

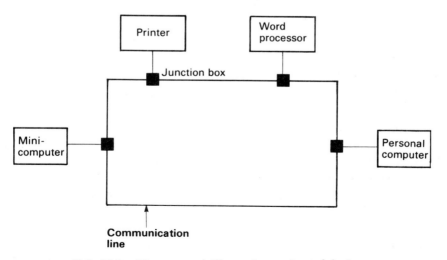

FIG. 19.1 *Ring network illustrating variety of devices*

'token passing rings'. *Tokens* are labelled packets of data continuously revolving around the ring – they have data written to and read from them continuously. The tokens can carry data between any computer on the network. This makes it necesary for each computer to constantly check tokens as they pass through their node. To ensure the signals sent from the transmitting machine are correctly received by the specified computer, the transmitting micro checks the token again as it passes through the network.

Failsafe Facilities
Various techniques are applied to basic ring structures to improve their performance and to prevent system degradation as a result of a fault on any terminal in the network. One technique is the provision of a *dual ring system* which has two circuits round the ring; one is the main circuit and the other provides fail-safe facilities. If the main circuit fails the standby circuit is automatically switched in to maintain continuity of operation. *Braiding systems* have three circuits, two of which are available in each direction from each terminal. The third circuit provides additional standby facilities in the event of a failure on any part of the ring.

IBM Token Ring
A ring network developed by IBM is known as the 'token ring local area network'. The token ring sends free tokens around the ring. A user has to wait until a free token arrives before transmitting data. The system is flexible because it is possible to increase the speed of transmission and incorporate additional users or new equipment at any location on the network pathway. This type of network can support up to 260 terminals. Signal boosters are necessary for dispersed networks with lengthy cabling needs. Speeds of 16 mbs (16,000,000 bits per second) are possible. The use of fibre optic cables, replacing twisted pair copper cables, may allow speeds of 100 mbs. It is also possible to connect mainframe computers on a token ring LAN either directly using a specially programmed personal computer or a minicomputer. Links are also facilitated via other gateways. Because data is in labelled packets the network can carry traffic using IBM's Systems Network Architecture protocols and the internationally accepted Open Systems Interconnection (OSI) protocols.

Star Network
Star networks have a central network controller or file server, usually

NETWORKS 217

a microcomputer controlling a disc drive, to which all nodes are connected. The network transmits data to specific nodes in accordance with the destination address. This type of network is used in timesharing systems whereby the central controller is a host computer to which all terminals are connected via modems (or acoustic couplers), multiplexors and telephone lines. If the central controller, whether a file server or central time sharing computer, breaks down the network ceases to function (*see* Fig. 19.2).

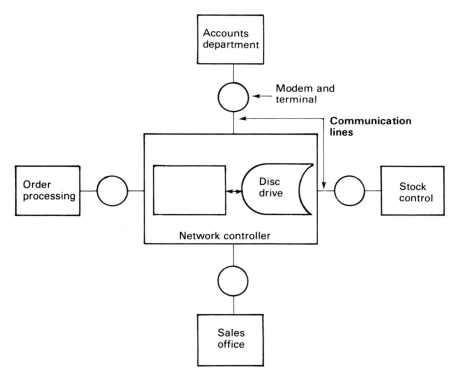

FIG. 19.2 *Star network*

BUS NETWORK

A bus is the term used to describe the communication line on which the various devices are connected by cable taps. Any device can be added to, or removed from, the network quite simply. Each device or node has a specific address and messages are routed to all nodes until the one to which the communication is addressed is reached. If one or several devices fail the network continues to function. Some bus networks have a system known as CSMA/CD, an abbreviation for Carrier Sense Multiple Access with Collision Detect. All terminals on the network listen to the carrier wave to detect if any other terminals are transmitting data. When two terminals listen simultaneously and each detect that transmissions are not occurring then they transmit data simultaneously, causing a collision of signals. Both terminals detect this situation by the Collision Detect facilities and wait for a short period of time before retransmitting the data (*see* Fig. 19.3).

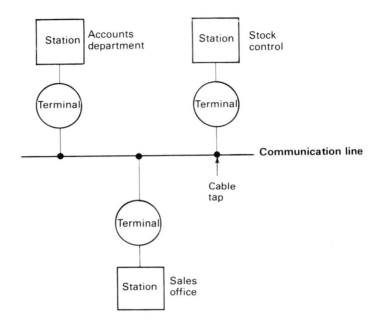

FIG. 19.3 *Bus network*

CLOSE-COUPLED NETWORKS

Each terminal in a close-coupled network has its own processor. Communication occurs on a bus which has a file-serving processor alongside the application processors, each of which is able to share any other's memory. The communication distances are very short which enables much faster transmission speeds to be achieved than in local area networks using coaxial or twisted-pair cables. The central processor does not poll each user's processor for detecting data to be transmitted but is 'demand' activated or 'interrupt driven'. The protocol to handle data transmissions is less complex than that required for LANs and the complex protocols for dealing with data collision and for ensuring the integrity of data are dispensed with.

VALUE-ADDED NETWORK

Value-added networks (VAN) provide additional services by third party vendors under a government licence. The additional services include automatic error detection and correction as well as 'Store and forward' message services, electronic mail and protocol conversions to access different computers and networks. The vendors can provide point to point or switched services on public telephone circuits providing they 'add value' to those circuits.

STORE AND FORWARD NETWORKS

The term store and forward relates to the temporary storage of messages in a computer system for later transmission. The system allows messages to be routed over networks which are not always accessible and requires one or more computer controlled exchanges (nodes) able to store messages and release them for onward transmission when a transmission path is available. By this means messages for different time zones can be 'stored and forwarded' to the destination during normal daytime.

WIDE AREA NETWORKS

Whereas local area networks provide the means of communication between offices in the same building, wide area networks provide facilities for communicating between geographically dispersed buildings. In such instances a business may distribute a number of computers in the various branches throughout the country linked to form a wide area network. These networks require data communication equipment such as modems and multiplexors and leased communication lines. LANs, on the other hand, do not need such facilities because they are in close proximity to each other and connected by internal cable. LANs may be connected to wide area networks by gateways.

SUMMARY OF KEY POINTS

- A network consists of interconnected computers and terminals which communicate with each other for the exchange of information.
- Networks facilitate distributed processing.
- Distributed processing provides local computing facilities in various business locations.

- A local area network (LAN) serves the needs of office or factory departments at the same location.
- LANs share resources such as printers and discs.
- LANs can be linked to other networks by gateways.
- Network topology includes ring, star and bus network structures.
- Other types of network include store and forward, wide area, close-coupled and value-added networks.

SELF-TEST QUESTIONS

1. Describe the features and purpose of a LAN.
2. What is distributed processing?
3. What resources are shared by network users?
4. What facilities are required to enable networks to function?
5. What function does a gateway serve?
6. Describe the characteristics of ring, star and bus network structures.
7. What advantages do close-coupled networks possess compared with LANs?
8. What are the features of value-added networks?
9. What benefits are provided by store and forward networks?
10. Explain the nature of wide area networks and state how they differ from local area networks.

FURTHER READING

Telecommunications primer, Graham Langley, (2edn) Pitman, London, 1986.

CHAPTER 20
What of the Future?

LEARNING OBJECTIVES

Information processing is a very hi-tech activity, belonging to an extremely volatile and dynamic technology—information technology. The first chapter provided an indication of the evolutionary nature of earlier information processing techniques, the text provides an outline of the current situation and this final chapter provides an outline of how communication and processing techniques will develop in the near future.

INTRODUCTION

Even with the most sophisticated developments and changes in information technology the essential purpose of information processing and information systems will remain unchanged.

Information will continue to be needed for the effective conduct of business operations. Management will also retain the need for information to facilitate their problem solving and decision making responsibilities. It remains vitally important, however, for management to be continually aware of the direction of technological developments in order to be forearmed and in a superior position to retain or obtain a competitive advantage.

COMPETITIVE ADVANTAGE

It is becoming increasingly necessary to integrate strategic planning with information planning because it is imperative that information processing systems optimise the use of technological resources in pursuit of corporate goals. Information is a valuable business resource but is a means to an end, not an end in itself. The value of information lies in how usefully it is applied in pursuit of goals which may be measured in terms of how well it provides a competitive advantage over the actions of competitors. This is ultimately expressed in the level of profit achieved by a business – the bottom line, as it is known. A lot depends upon how closely information flows are linked to the competitive situation. Computer communication links are being installed between manufacturers and suppliers to attain more control over the flow of essential raw materials into their automated manufacturing processes. This is of direct relevance to the quest for higher productivity because it results in lower costs and prices which, if passed on to customers, increase competitiveness. Product distributors are also tending to implement order entry terminals at customers' locations so that orders can be entered directly into the distributor's computer, speeding up the process of order handling. These are examples of what are becoming known as 'added value' applications because the technology adds value to products or services.

In addition, the markets of many industries are becoming more widespread, even global, and therefore requiring efficient telecommunications to reduce the reaction time of responses to international enquiries. The level of customer service is also improved.

FIFTH GENERATION COMPUTERS

The latest breed of computers under development will be complex knowledge-based systems with in-built artificial intelligence using languages such as Lisp and Prolog. The latter feature symbol manipulating and logic programming facilities. They will be capable of being addressed in natural language, simplifying their use by non-specialists. They will also incorporate pattern recognition and speech synthesis allowing business documents to be produced directly from the input of human speech. They will translate foreign languages from one language to another automatically which will improve international communications. A Japanese computer under development is said to have a potential capability of achieving 250 thousand logical inferences per second (250 KLIPS). Another Japanese computer, referred to as a parallel inference machine with 100 processing elements, has a potential speed of 10 to 20 million logical inferences per second (MLIPS). This provides some idea of the speed of future computers.

COMMUNICATIONS

Networks
As the incidence of communications between computers has increased it has created a mixture of many incompatible communication networks. This situation is predicted to remain in existence in the

foreseeable future. Increasing pressure, however, is being applied to integrate the diverse systems into global networks for the purpose of maximising their efficiency and optimising the investment in the resources. A major problem to the attainment of such a degree of integration is the lack of protocol standards* as the protocols of various vendors (suppliers of communication equipment) are incompatible. This situation is likely to change over the next ten years as a move towards standard communication protocols gains momentum. There exists a gradual move towards the adoption of OSI (Open Systems Interconnect) standards. The OSI standards include MAP (Manufacturing Automation Protocol) and TOP (Technical Office Protocol).

Transmission of Digital Data

The transmission of data will increasingly be digital rather than analogue. Analogue transmission consists of electrical wave forms of varying amplitude representing for example the pattern of the human voice. Analogue transmission has been in use for many years as the basis of telephone technology and is very effective for this purpose, but it is not so suitable for high speed data transmission. When using telephone lines for transmitting data from a terminal to a computer, the digital signals from the terminal need to be converted to analogue signals by an acoustic coupler or modem (modulator/demodulator). When the signals are received by the distant computer the signals are reconverted to digital form by a modem, prior to being input to the computer for processing. Digital transmission consists of electrical pulses representing data in binary code as a series of on/off pulses, in the same manner as a computer system. Digital compared to analogue technology has a number of advantages; higher transmission speed; lower incidence of errors; and the capability to mix data, voice, image and text on the same circuit. A new network structure is being introduced known as Integrated Services Digital Network (ISDN).

Fibre Optic Transmission Lines

Fibre optics are transparent glass reads or strands, each as fine as a human hair, capable of handling more than one thousand telephone conversations simultaneously. They allow data to be transmitted at high speed, have a high signal capacity and are unaffected by electri-

---

* The term protocol relates to the procedures, agreements and rules governing the way information flows in a system between transmitting and receiving devices. A protocol includes such matters as the format of messages, the sequence or ordering of events and the responses and actions which can be performed by each user.

cal interference. It is for these reasons that fibre optic lines are replacing coaxial and twisted pair cable in local area networks (LANs).

Satellite Transmission
Roof top dishes for satellite communications are likely to replace surface lines to transmit large volumes of data at high speed between dispersed locations and a central computer facility. This applies to retail organisations, for instance, having many branches needing to transmit transaction data to head office each day or at more frequent intervals. The control of merchandise is improved by avoiding excessive stocks and shortages. Managers are also regularly provided with information relating to sales turnover and profitability, allowing more effective management and decision-making.

Value Added Data Services (VADS)
VADS are public data network services with added value services including protocol conversion, electronic data interchange (EDI), viewdata systems and managed network services. VADS can only be supplied under licence from the government and it is necessary to conform to OSI standards. VADS benefit users with large volumes of data to be transferred between locations and the services have been used by many types of operation including public health services, financial services and the motor trade.

IMAGE PROCESSING

Visual Information Systems: Interactive Video
There is likely to be an expansion in interactive video applications in future as such systems can provide an impressive impact in the visual display of information. The heart of an interactive video system is an optical video disc which can store more than 50000 high quality colour pictures per side. When controlled by a computer the videodisc player can locate any picture instantly and display stills, motion pictures or a combination of both. The image displayed on the screen can include text or graphics stored in the computer's memory. Such systems may be used to display product details to customers, for learning programmes and industrial training. Many types of audio-visual material can be recorded on the disc including film, videotape, photostills, microfilm, printed text and computer printouts, etc. Flexible systems which allow updating of multi-media information require digital imaging and audio technologies to complement analogue videodisc technology.

DESK-TOP PUBLISHING

Desk-top publishing is becoming widely used because of its relative simplicity compared with the skill and experience required for traditional publishing. The application of specialist software allows a personal computer to be used as a publishing and design tool facilitating the production of top-quality publications. The screen of the computer acts as an electronic pasteboard complete with rules, column guides and various design aids. Pull-down menus are used for selecting options and a mouse is used for selection and manipulation of text, graphics and menu commands. Complete control is obtained of page composition including the integration of text and graphics from many sources by means of desk-top image scanners. Such systems have built-in text editing facilities for inserting, deleting, cutting, pasting or creating new text.

OPERATING SYSTEMS

The Real-time Operating System Nucleus (TRON)

TRON, being developed in Japan, is a concept which aims to provide a standard approach to business problems for the 1990s. It attempts to create specifications for microcomputer interfaces in an 'open' environment which could lead to worldwide standards for microcomputers for the next decade. Various versions are envisaged including those for industry and others for data interchange between intelligent devices in a network and a version for controlling wide area networks.

ARTIFICIAL INTELLIGENCE

The application of knowledge based systems (expert systems) is likely to gain momentum as their usefulness for problem solving becomes apparent. An expert system simulates human knowledge by making deductions from given facts using the rules of logical inference. It also has the capability of justifying its line of reasoning to the user of the system. An expert system consists of three primary elements—an inference engine which acts as a rule interpreter; a knowledge base which is the heart of the system containing rules; and a database storing details relating to the status of the system and facts relating to a particular domain or subject area. In the business context subject areas include an advisor for credit card applications to assess the creditworthiness of an applicant or variations of this type of application relating to mortgage or loan applications. In the medical area they are sometimes used to help doctors make a diagnosis of a disease.

PROGRAM GENERATORS

Program generators are program builders consisting of software designed to allow non-computer specialists to develop their own application programs because their use is less complex than writing a program in a high-level programming language. They may also be usefully employed by experienced programmers because the software generates the equivalent of several statements which speeds up the process of program development. A program generator may be used to develop traditional business applications such as payroll, accounts, invoicing and stock control. A generator can also be used to develop programs for applications where package programs are unavailable.

OFFICE SUPPORT SYSTEMS

Office support systems are likely to be more widely used in the future because they support office functions enabling them to accomplish tasks in a more efficient manner. Office support systems include electronic mail for speeding up inter-office communications; electronic filing of documents for speeding up the process of filing and retrieval of documents; word processing for improving the preparation, storage and retrieval of reports and other text and eliminating unnecessary duplication of documents by means of magnetically stored standard letters and/or standard paragraphs, etc.

INFORMATION CENTRE

Information centres are becoming increasingly common in industry: their prime function is to provide computer training enabling end-users to perform personal computing activities, and facilities for downloading data from a database for local processing on a personal computer by an end-user.

DECISION SUPPORT SYSTEMS

Decision support systems will probably be used more extensively because they provide executives with the tools for processing data to be used for problem solving and decision making. The tools include a query language for accessing a database; software for extracting data from the files of the mainframe computer for transfer to the user's computer; software for defining new records; a report writer and decision support system including programs for spreadsheets, business modelling, statistical analysis, data manipulation and graphics. This type of facility extends the prowess of executives as they are able to perform processing tasks previously performed by specialised personnel in the centralised computer facility. Alternatively, in the absence of computing facilities, tasks were performed very laboriously by slide rule or pocket calculator which required time and patience. Decision support software enables information to be structured, analysed and modelled to assist in the decision-making process. It provides the framework for breaking down a problem into its constituent elements. Decision modelling evaluates a series of options against a set of criteria in order to determine the best. The software enables criteria to be defined by the user and weighted in terms of their importance. The user's options are then analysed against the criteria, and the software then ranks them in terms of best overall fit. In addition, sensitivity or what if? analyses can be carried out by changing values and weightings. Results can be examined in summary form to compare and contrast the pros and cons of both sides. The software allows the user to re-organise and modify information by following logical paths around the model. The various options provided by the software are accessed by means of pull-down menus and function keys.

SUMMARY OF KEY POINTS

- It is becoming increasingly necessary to integrate strategic planning with information planning, to optimise the use of technological resources in pursuit of corporate goals.
- Added-value applications are those which add value to products or services.
- Efficient telecommunications are required for effectively dealing with widespread international business operations.
- The future generation of computers will be complex knowledge-based systems with in-built artificial intelligence.
- Digital transmission of data will increase in the future.
- Fibre optic transmission lines will replace coaxial and twisted pair cable in LANs.
- There is likely to be an expansion in the use of interactive video applications.
- Desk-top publishing will become widely applied because of its relative ease of use by the non-professional.

- There will be a tendency to develop more powerful operating systems and attempts to standardise them internationally.
- Greater degree of software integration for combining wordprocessing, spreadsheet, database, graphics and report writing combined with application development languages.

SELF-TEST QUESTIONS

1. What do you understand by the term 'competitive advantage' and how does it relate to the value of information?
2. Why are computer intercommunication links being installed between manufacturers and suppliers and between distributors and customers?
3. What developments are likely to occur in the field of information technology?

FURTHER READING

Trends in information technology, Sunday Times and Arthur Andersen & Co, London, 1988.

APPENDIX:
Case Studies

CASE STUDY 1

The Problem
The office manager of ABC Plastics plc is responsible for postal services, circulation of internal memos and the internal telephone system. He has received complaints from personnel in various departments regarding memos going adrift. This is creating uncoordinated relationships between personnel in inter-related functions which is causing a failure to make important decisions.

The office manager is also aware of the situation which prevails and the frustration created when executives fail to establish contact on the internal telephone system because of the absence of the person being called or due to the line being engaged.

The managing director has requested the office manager to propose a solution to these problems.

The Solution
The office manager is keen to apply appropriate modern information technology techniques and facilities when he considers there is a good reason to implement them. In this instance he is aware of the features of electronic mail and informs the managing director of the following details in a report.

General Features of Electronic Mail Systems
Electronic mail is a technique for electronically distributing mail (messages) which has been prepared and transmitted by a personal computer. This facility can dispense with the internal circulation of memos by normal internal mail distribution methods; in many instances it can also dispense with the use of the internal telephone system. Indeed it is possible to dispense with external postal services in some instances, as will be outlined below. When a message is created on the sender's system it is electronically delivered to the receiver's system. The receiver reads the document on a video screen exactly as it was transmitted electronically. Electronic mail facilities may be incorporated in Local Area Networks or may be provided by a public service such as the Dialcom Electronic Mail service provided

by Telecom Gold supported by British Telecom. Digital PABX telephone exchanges, which form a catalyst for the electronic office as a whole, allow access to local area networks, computers, and peripheral devices such as printers as well as other office equipment such as telex machines. Messages can be transmitted to any location providing the device at the location and the sending device can be connected to the telephone system.

Advantages of Electronic Mail
Electronic mail has a number of advantages over normal postal services, one of which is its speed of transmission (which is much faster than the time it takes for mail to be delivered by postal services). With the normal postal service important mail may delayed or even lost, which can have drastic consequences to the business—perhaps resulting in important orders being lost. Electronic mail eliminates the delay in a recipient receiving a message because it is immediately stored in the memory of the recipient's computer. A delay does occur, of course, when the recipient is out of the office. Electronic mail has a number of advantages over the normal telephone system: for instance a person does not have to be present at the time a message is transmitted by electronic mail but does have to be present to receive a phone call. Also, if the recipient of a message is using the telephone when someone sends him a message on electronic mail, the message is stored on the recipient's computer. This is much more efficient than one manager telephoning a colleague and finding that the telephone is continuously engaged.

Telecom Gold
This electronic system provides a number of facilities such as an electronic diary, word processing, a range of compilers for different languages as well as electronic mail. The system is used by thousands of people using either the telephone with 300 or 1200 bps modems or via the PSS (packet switching service). The system has six Prime computers on the international Dialcom network.

It is necessary for a subscriber to 'LOG IN' to the system by entering the relevant user ID, which consists of three letters identifying the user group followed by three digits for identifying the member of the group. A password also has to be entered; this is not displayed for security reasons. If the user ID and password are accepted, the user is allowed access to the system. A 'mailbox' is allocated to each user which is labelled with the users's ID. The mailbox is a section of the computer's internal memory which stores messages. The command

MAIL when entered connects the user to the electronic mail system. The computer then expects the user to enter a command which can be either SEND, READ or SCAN. When SEND is entered the computer indicates that it requires the user to state the IDs of the recipients of the message to be sent. The READ command allows the user to read the whole of a message but SCAN only lists the sender of the message, the time, date, who the message was from and a single line describing the message content. If there are no message stores for a user then the response to a READ or SCAN command is 'no mail at present'. Messages can be transmitted to a number of recipients without any physical reproduction being necessary, which is an advantage over the normal system of correspondence where a copy has to be reproduced for each recipient. This allows all nodes (all PC's for instance) in a local area network to receive the same message, if relevant.

Prestel's Electronic Mail Service
This service, known as Mailbox, is accessible by a large proportion of telephone users on a local call basis. Each Prestel client has a Mailbox which is the electronic equivalent of a pigeonhole for storing letters in a normal postal service. The service maintains an alphabetical directory of clients which is updated every week. The way in which Mailbox functions is to call up PRESTEL in the usual way, select a message page from the Mailbox index, enter the recipient's Mailbox number and any message. The page is then transmitted. The message is stored in the addressee's Mailbox and the person is informed of messages awaiting them the next time they are in contact with Prestel. Any number of messages can be stored in the Mailbox for any length of time. The system provides for a wide selection of page designs including memo layouts and standard message layouts.

Conclusions
Electronic mail will not be suitable for all ABC plastic's business communications or document handling needs. It is not suitable for dealing with documents requiring an authorising signature, for long texts or for photographs. However, it does allow day-to-day communication to be conducted far more efficiently than at present and will eliminate the problem of memos going astray as well as allowing busy managers to leave messages for one another.

CASE STUDY 2

The Problem
Kettles Incorporated is an expanding company which manufactures domestic electrical appliances including electric kettles, fires, percolators, refrigerators and irons. It markets these through wholesale distributors and has now achieved a 50% share of the Home market. The chief accountant finds the current manual accounting system unwieldy and inefficient because of business growth, which is increasing at the rate of 20% per annum. The result of this is to delay the despatch of invoices and statements of account which is causing cash flow problems and late month end accounts. Management are displeased with this situation and require monthly accounts to be available five days after the month end. The accounting system is inefficient despite employing more staff on the various accounting activities. The chief accountant has discussed the situation with the general manager who has requested the systems department to conduct a feasibility study and provide a proposal to improve the performance of the accounting system as a whole, to avoid the need to increase the number of staff, to improve cash flow to avoid unnecessary bank overdrafts and to produce monthly accounts by the due date.

The Solution
The following details outline a proposal to streamline the accounting function. Because the accounting function is an important business activity with a high volume information processing commitment it is proposed that a dedicated, small but powerful business computer be implemented combined with a sophisticated integrated accounting software package.

The Integrated Accounting Package
An integrated accounting package consists of a suite of interrelated programs often of modular structure. Each module can be run separately or in combination with others on an integrated basis. Accounting packages typically include modules for sales, purchase and nominal ledgers, invoicing, stock control, payroll and costing. Integrated packages streamline the accounting routines by transferring common transaction data from one application module to another. This avoids having to input the same data more than once. Some packages are designed to run on a single user basis but others are designed as multi-user systems, using concurrent operating systems. The applications

are usually menu driven and 'user friendly' because they guide the user through each processing stage by means of prompts. Some packages are designed for the small business and others for the larger business.

Before running an integrated accounting package the system will have to be tailored to suit the needs of Kettles Incorporated: the default parameters must be redefined as they are included initially on the basis of a standard set of business characteristics. Most systems are interactive requiring the user and the computer to intercommunicate by exchanging messages at various stages of processing.

An important requirement is to copy the master programs to other discs as a safeguard against theft or damaging them as a result of a disc malfunction or corrupting them by accidental overwriting.

Some package suppliers allow their packages to be used in a limited way for a trial period. It is necessary to phone the supplier to obtain a security code to provide a key to access the software which prevent programs being used by unauthorised users. When the code is typed in, a menu is displayed for selecting the desired option according to the routine required to be processed.

When setting up the system Kettles Incorporated must decide whether to use pre-printed or blank stationery.

It is also necessary to make a decision when to change the system from that presently in operation. The best time to change over is usually the beginning of a financial year because balances need to be brought forward each year in respect of debtors, creditors and fixed assets, regardless of the method of accounting employed.

All accounting systems should be structured on the basis of an effective coding structure specified in a 'Chart of accounts' covering expense, customer, supplier, nominal ledger, departmental (cost centre). The various codes facilitate data transfers and postings between ledgers.

The nominal ledger is the central hub of an accounting package to which all transaction summaries are posted from the other modules. The main menu of a typical nominal ledger may contain details as shown below:

Post transactions to nominal ledger
Account period end processing
End of year processing
Report production
System maintenance
Master file maintenance
Enquiry processing

If the 'Post transactions to nominal ledger' option is selected a submenu containing the following details will be displayed:

Automatic posting
Post journals and accruals

The system may ask if the transaction is a debit or credit; it may also enquire whether the entry is correct, to which the user responds by typing Y for yes, or N for no. If the entry is incorrect it is then necessary to make the appropriate correction: a control key with a character key may clear the current entry or the new entry may overwrite the previous one. Each time data is entered it is stored ready for printing out on a schedule for the provision of an audit trail. A message is then displayed which asks if there are any more transactions, to which the response is Y for yes, or N for no. If the response is N the system reverts to the 'main menu' for the selection of other options. The nominal ledger is updated with the relevant transactions by nominal ledger code in respect of items such as: stock transactions, sales and purchases; plant and machinery acquisitions and depreciation; cash; and payroll details.

If the 'Account period end processing' option is selected a submenu containing the following details will be displayed:

File security
Trial balance
Print balance sheet
Print profit and loss account
Print operating statement
Close period

In accordance with the selected option, a trial balance, profit and loss account or balance sheet is printed. The profit and loss account typically contains details relating to: the value of sales, the cost of sales, wages, salaries, establishment charges, administrative expenses, depreciation, selling and distribution expenses, gross and net profit. A balance sheet is printed which contains entries for share capital, capital reserves, and current liabilities including creditors and bank overdrafts. Fixed assets are recorded including the value of buildings and plant and machinery less depreciation, the value of stock, debtors and cash.

Some nominal ledger systems maintain for every account the budgeted and actual values for each period in the current financial year. The annual budget for each expense can be entered manually for every period in the financial year or the expenses can be spread automatically over all the periods from the total budget figure.

Some packages provide for account enquiries during data entry activities. The screen displays all the account details and a printout is provided if required.

The invoicing module normally provides for price selection, terms of trade and discounts. Provision is also made for variable rates of tax. When items are despatched to a customer an invoice is produced which contains information for updating the sales ledger; the quantities despatched are updated on the stock file which provides data for stock management.

A typical sales ledger module has a number of facilities including;

Open-item method for customer accounts (items outstanding)
List of debtors by age of debt
Statements of account

When an invoice is entered the customer's credit is automatically checked and a debtor control list shows accounts with an overdue balance or when a credit limit has been exceeded. A warning is displayed on the screen of any account which is overdue. In such instances letters of increasing severity can be automatically printed and sent to the customer. Integration with a word processing package is provided for in some instances utilising the name and address file for printing these standard letters.

Cash receipts can be fully or partially allocated to invoices. Selecting the month-end routine from the main menu clears all fully paid transactions leaving only the outstanding balances.

Some payroll modules convert the data recorded on payslips into the file format required by the Bank Automatic Clearing Service (BACS). The data can be transmitted via modem directly to the bank's computer installation or recorded on floppy disc and sent through the post. Or it can be delivered by hand. When the data has been accepted, salaries and wages can be paid directly into the individual employee's bank account.

The purchase ledger module typically provides for the following requirements:

Open-item accounting
Aged list of account balances
Random enquiry facilities
Remittance advices
Preparation of cheques and credit transfers
Automatic listing of cheques due for payment based on pre-established credit period

Mail shots
Cash discounts (after agreement with supplier)

For audit control purposes most packages print out details of transactions including: the value and number of invoices; value and number of credits; and cash transactions.

Typical packages also provide for the creation of back-up files for security as part of the end of posting routine. Prompts from the program inform the user when to load the discs for copying purposes.

Most packages allow the printing of reports of various types, the details for which can be stored on a spooling file. This allows a print run to be implemented as one task at a suitable time after the processing is completed.

Benefits
Benefits include the reduction in the number of staff concerned with accounting routines, increased accuracy of processing, faster reporting and the facility for updating master files on a transaction basis as they occur.

Current business software incorporates multi-windowing, multi-lingual and multi-currency conversion facilities. 4th Generation Language techniques are used allowing flexibility of screen design and print layout. As an example, a payroll clerk may design a simple screen layout to assist the entry of hours worked on different jobs by employees for job costing. For this purpose the clerk would use a window to access data from a job costing module. The accountant, by using other windows, is able to inspect job costing information on particular jobs or the status of a particular overhead expense. Designing screens and personalised menus to operate them is accomplished by an edit program. This level of sophistication provides untold benefits particularly in multi-national companies as screens on the same system can be displayed in different languages. This facility enables subsidiary companies to input information in the screen formats designed for their specific use.

Software Related to Computer Configuration
Before selecting a computer Kettles Incorporated must decide upon the type of integrated software required: its effectiveness, its price and its source. Software is designed to run on specific models, using a defined operating system and a minimum RAM requirement. These factors are provided in literature supplied by the company which developed the software or from an authorised dealer. Having

determined the software requirement it is necessary to select a computer configuration on which the software has been proved to run satisfactorily.

CASE STUDY 3

The Problem
The Steelbridge engineering company has a head office in London with a large computer in a centralised data/information processing department serving the information processing needs of three branch works. The branch works are located in Birmingham, Wolverhampton and Glasgow. Each branch has a number of terminals connected to the head office computer. The data processing commitment under such circumstances is becoming unwieldy and the terminals are subjected to increasing delays because of increasing traffic density on the transmission lines. Each branch transmits payroll data to the head office computer for processing which prints payrolls and payslips and bank giros for employees. These are sent through the post to the respective branches. The branches also transmit to the head office accounting data relating to purchases, sales, costs and overheads for preparing both branch and consolidated accounts by the head office computer. Management requires the system development staff to conduct a feasibility study for the purpose of proposing a more effective alternative arrangement.

The details which follow provide the framework of such a proposal for an alternative configuration which will meet the approval of management.

The Proposal
A proposal to eliminate the weaknesses of the current system is the installation of a minicomputer at each of the branch works, applying the principles of distributed processing to replace centralised processing. The payroll and accounting departments in each of the branch works are already equipped with terminals for transmitting data to the head office. These may be used to input data for processing by their own local computer. This will be facilitated by a distributed database storing payroll and accounting records for each branch. The central computer can be employed for processing head office data relating to payroll, estimating, sales forecasting, running corporate simulation models, preparation of budgets and the production of consolidated accounts. The central computer, if considered appropriate,

238 BUSINESS SYSTEMS AND INFORMATION TECHNOLOGY

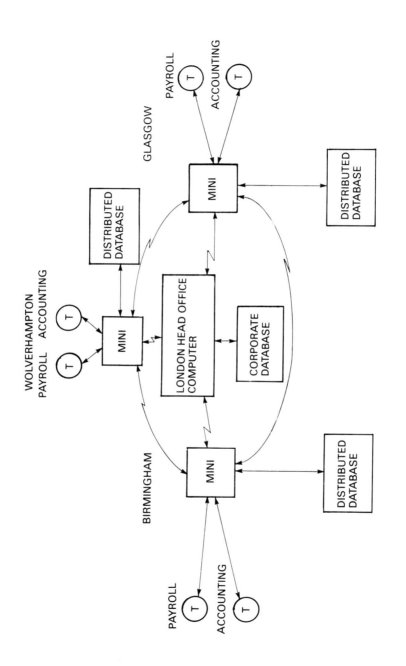

FIG. A.1

can act as host to the distributed systems providing corporate information by means of a central database. The accounting details stored in the local databases can be transmitted to the head office computer's database for accounting consolidations. All the branches will be connected by transmission lines to allow data transfers between them. Figure A.1 shows the arrangement. This arrangement will relieve the pressure on the central facilities and improve the flow of information throughout the business. In such a proposal it is necessary to consider the hardware and software costs and compare them with the expected benefits in order to ensure it is financially acceptable.

An alternative scheme to that outlined involves the installation of a much larger computer capable of handling terminal operations more effectively. It will therefore be necessary to compare the total cost of a larger central computer system with the total cost of the proposed system which includes the cost of three minicomputers. There is no need to incur additional costs by buying terminals as they are already in use for transmitting data to the head office and will be used to input data to the local computer in the proposed system. Retaining the existing computer as host to the distributed network will not incur additional costs except for those relating to system development and the cost of software for network control.

CASE STUDY 4

The Problem
A new manager has been appointed to the Mail Order Bookshop. Appalled by the existing order processing system (which is basically a cardboard box on the floor which is overflowing with old orders) she proposes to introduce more modern systems.

The Proposal
The following details relate to the processing routine for a proposed order processing application. Orders are received from customers in the order department. These are then checked by the order clerk, who computes an approximate value of the order by multiplying the quantity of each item by its price and adding all the values. This value is checked against the customer's account. If payments from the customer have been delayed or the account balance is in excess of the credit limit then the order is not accepted without confirmation from the credit controller in conjunction with the sales manager. This pro-

cedure is important because even though it is essential for a business to make sales, it is also essential that payment is received for the goods supplied as otherwise the business will suffer from a shortage of cash to finance its operations. If the customer's credit is satisfactory, the stock is checked to assess stock availability. Stock records are adjusted (updated) by deducting the quantities sent to the customers from the quantity in stock so that the records show the current stock position. Eventually the stock is increased when new supplies are received in the warehouse. Shortages are recorded on a shortage list which is sent to the buying office to replenish the items obtained from outside suppliers.

Order details including adjustments for stock shortages are sent to the data preparation section for encoding onto magnetic disc prior to processing by computer. It is essential that only the quantity of items available is recorded on the despatch note and invoices because it is important to ensure that the correct quantity is charged to the customer—not the quantity ordered. A copy of the despatch note is sent to the customer with the goods. The invoice is sent to the customer and the invoice value is recorded (updated) on the customer's account in the sales ledger. A day book is prepared listing all the sales transactions.

At the end of the trading period, i.e. the end of the calendar month, it is normal practice to produce statements of account from details on each customer's account in the sales ledger.

Prior to allowing the manager to implement his new system, the owners of The Mail Order Bookshop require her to:

1 List the forms used for recording initial data
2 List and explain the documents produced by the application
3 List the clerical activities in the order department
4 List data preparation operations
5 List the computer processing operations
6 Construct a system flowchart of the application including clerical, data preparation and computer activities.

Her analysis is as follows:

1 *Forms for recording initial data*
   a Sales order originated by the customer
   b Internal order originated by the order clerk

2 *Documents produced*
   a Shortage report: prepared by order clerk and sent to the buying office to inform them of items needing replenishment.

b Purchase order: originated by the buying office from shortage report to instruct suppliers of items required.
   c Despatch note: sent with the goods to the customer. Informs the customer of goods received which can be matched with the order copy.
   d Invoice: sent to the customer to charge for the goods despatched.
   e Day book: a list of invoice values is produced for accounting and auditing.
   Statements of account: for informing customers of the amount owing for goods received on credit showing an age analysis of amounts outstanding.
   f Error report consisting of invalid order details.

3 *Clerical operations*
   a Calculate value of orders.
   b Check credit.
   c Check stock, report shortages and record despatches on the relevant record in the stock file (update stock file).

4 *Data preparation operations*
   Data on the order forms is encoded to magnetic disc by a key-to-disc system producing the orders file.

5 *Computer Processing operations*
   a Input and validate orders for completeness and correctness. Print error report.
   b Sort orders file to customer account number sequence.
   c Compute invoice values, store on valued orders file and print daybook listing.
   d Print despatch note and invoices and update customer account.
   e Print statement of account and accounts list and send statements to customer.

6 The flow chart the manager prepares is shown in Fig. A2.

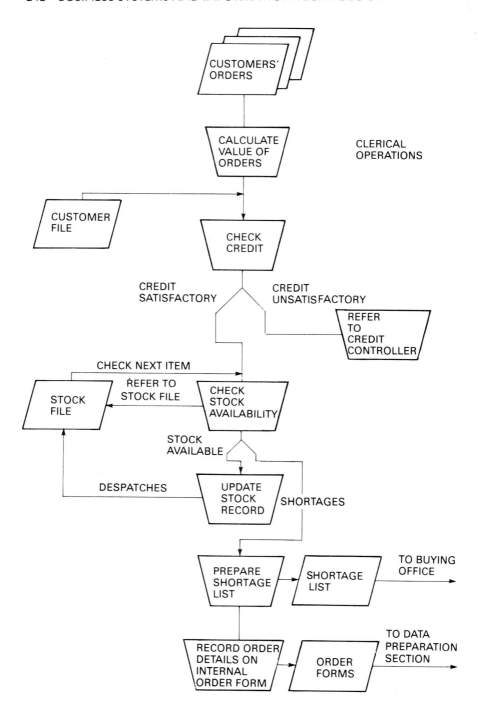

CASE STUDIES 243

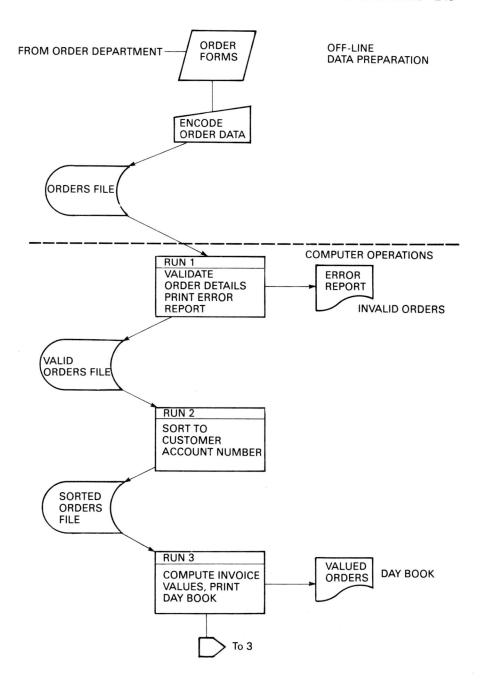

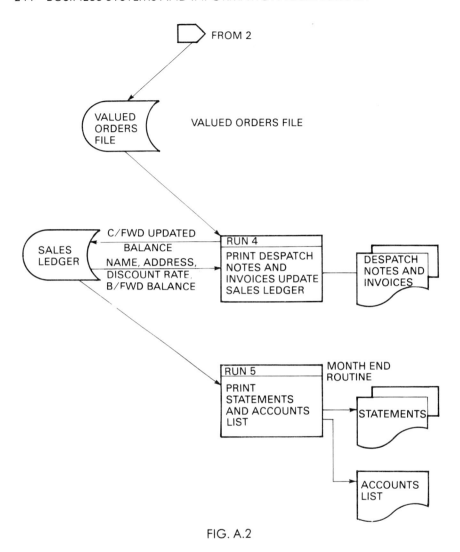

FIG. A.2

CASE STUDY 5

The Problem

Got-It-All is a multiple retailer whose volume of business is expanding very quickly. The owner realises he must obtain larger premises to convert his business into a walkaround supermarket. His current business activities have used old-type cash registers for recording sales to customers. The retailer appreciates that a more sophisticated check-out system will be necessary not only to speed up the flow of customers through the supermarket but also to provide information on sales to assess daily profitability and information on stocks for efficient stock management. He has contacted a computer manufacturer who sends Got-It-All a report on the benefits of Point of Sale systems.

The Report
In Point of Sale retail systems, details of customer's purchases (sales) are recorded (captured) by laser scanners at check-out points. A scanner senses data encoded as a *bar code* on the label of the product, which may be a pack of bacon, a loaf of bread, a tin of beans, or a specially weighed pack of potatoes. There are several bar codes including the American Universal Product code (AUP) and the European Article Numbering code (EAN). The light and dark lines of the code are converted by the scanner into a digital number which is sent to the in-store minicomputer. The computer looks up the number on the disc file and transfers it to the memory of the computer and then transmits the price of the item to the check-out terminal. The price is visually displayed to enable the customer to verify it. The price and description of the commodity are printed onto the customer's receipt together with the total amount, the cash received and the amount of change. Other printed details include the date and check-out number for reference purposes in case of a query. Although not in wide use a system has been developed which speaks the prices for customers. The digitised sounds are stored in a magnetic memory and audio responses are given on receipt of instructions from a bar code reader.

The equipment required to operate this type of system includes:

a Retail terminals at each check-out point which can function as free standing sales registers equipped with a laser bar code scanner.
b A keyboard and VDU as back-up in the event of a malfunction with the bar code scanner.
c An in-store minicomputer supporting the terminals at the various check-out points.
d A printer for printing customer receipts.
e A data communication link including modems if the system is linked to banks for electronic fund transfers. This would also be used for credit checking.
f Some systems have facilities for optical scanning of OCR (optical character recognition) fonts and magnetic card readers for credit card processing.

The advantages of Point of Sale systems to the shopper are as follows:

a More efficient check-out service as customers do not spend so much time queueing at peak times.

b Itemised till receipts providing a visible check on the charged goods and their price.

The advantages of point-of-sale systems to Got-It-All would be:

a More efficient stores administration reducing the number of staff required to staff check-out points.

b Much more information can be obtained from this type of system including sales turnover trends, gross and net margins, forward purchasing commitments, slow moving and fast moving stocks (stock velocity ratios), all of which assist in improving efficiency and profitability.

INDEX

4GL, *see* Fourth generation language

Accounting packages, *see* Integrated accounting packages
Accounting systems, 14
Acoustic coupler, 8
Adaptive learning, 203
Adding new fields, database, 191, 192
Adding new records, database, 182, 190
Address bus, 43
Address generations, algorithmic, 65–67
Addressing machine, 4
Algorithmic address generation, 65–67
Alternative key, 31
ALU, *see* arithmetic/logic unit
Amendment, records, 81
Application packages, *see* Applications software
Application programs, 46
Applications, microcomputer, 127
Applications software, 137–212
Arithmetic/logic unit (ALU), 42
Article numbering, 245
Artificial intelligence, 225
ASCII, 41
Asset records, database, 177–187
Attribute, 31, 181, 182, 193
Attributes, computer, 56, 57
AUP, 245
Automated approach, 104

BACS, 235
Backing storage devices, 123, 130
Backward chaining, 207
Bar code, 245
Batch processing, 120–124
Batch processing configuration, 123, 124
Benchmark tests, 52, 53
Benefits, computer, 57
Benefits, information technology, 89
Binary digit, 41
Bits, 41
Block diagram, 106, 107
Braiding systems, 216
Bubble sorting, 70
Bus, 43
Bus network, 217, 218
Business models, *see* modelling
Business systems, 11–15
Byte, 41, 43

Calculating, 33
Capital expenditure, 55, 56
CASE tools, 104
Central processing unit (CPU), 42–44, 124, 130

Chaining, 207
Channels, 43
Characters, 41, 42
Close-coupled network, 218
Collecting knowledge, 200, 201
Command file, database, 186, 196–199
Command selection keys, 87
Communication equipment, 124, 130
Communications, 222–224
Comparator, 29
Comparing, 34
Competitive advantage, 221, 222
Computations, 123
Computer attributes, 56, 57
Computer benefits, 51
Computer configuration, 42, 123, 124
Computer program, 46
Computer run chart, 110
Computer selection, 50–57
Computerised information systems, 29
Computerised stock control, *see* Inventory control system
Conceptual model, 96, 131, 132
Console, 124, 130
Construction of system flowcharts, 110, 111
Context diagram, 96, 98
Control bus, 43
Control unit, 42
Controlling, 35
Coordination of functions, 16
CP/M, 45
CPU, *see* Central processing unit
Customer data, 139
Cybernetic control process, *see* Feedback *and* Homeostasis
Cylinder concept, 81, 82

Data, 30
Database, 6, 165–199
   adding new fields, 191, 192
   adding new records, 182, 190
   command files, 186, 196–199
   deleting records, 185, 186, 190, 191
   file copying, 189
   file creation, 178, 188
   file updating, 75–81, 127
   finding a record, 84, 193, 194
   indexing, 183, 184, 193
   personnel records, 187–199
   relational, 166–168
Database application, 173
Database host, *see* Public database
Database management system (DBMS), 173
Database query system, *see* Query language
Database structures, 166–170

248 INDEX

Database types, *see* Database structures *and* Public databases
Data bus, 43
Data conversion, 28
Data description language (DDL), 173
Data dictionary, 172, 173
Data flow, 98
Data flow diagram, 99
Data independence, 172
Data modelling, 99
Data preparation devices, 123
Data storage, *see* Backing storage
Data validation, *see* Validating
Data verification, *see* Verifying
dBASE III+, 173–175
DBMS, *see* Database management system
DDL, *see* Data description language
Decision support systems, 226, 227
Decision tables, *see* Knowledge based systems
Deleting records, database, 185, 186, 190, 191
Deletion, records, 81
Delivery labels, 141
Delivery note, 140
Desk-top publishing, 225
Development costs, 56
Development tools, knowledge based system, 208, 209
Deviations, 29
Device independence, 172
Dialogue, 86–91
Dictionary, *see* Data dictionary
Digital data, 223
Digital PABX, 7
Digits, 3, 41
Direct access, 64–67
Direct machine environment (DME), 145
Disc file updating, 78–81
Disc storage, *see* Backing storage devices
Display, records, 85, 86, 194
Distributed processing, 6, 237–239
DME, *see* Direct machine environment
Domain experts, *see* Knowledge based systems
Drop-down menus, 91
Dual ring system, 216

EAN, 245
EBCDIC, 41
Economic environment, 16
Effective systems, need for, 17
Effector, 29
Electronic calculators, 4
Electronic computers, 41–48
Electronic diary, 7
Electronic executive office, home-based, 7, 8
Electronic filing, 6
Electronic funds transfer, 245
Electronic mail, 6, 229–231
Electronic office, 7, 8
Electric technology, 3
Elements of a computer system, 41–44
Elements of a control system, *see* Feedback *and* Homeostasis
End of session processing, 142, 143
Entity, 30, 31
Entity diagram, 99
Entity life history diagram, 96
Error signal, 29
Evolution of electronic technology, 3–6
Exception principle, 29
Expert system, *see* Knowledge based system

Failsafe facilities, networks, 216
Feasibility study, 50–52
Feasibility study report, 51
Feedback, 29
Fibre optics, 223–224
Field, 31
Fifth generation computers, 222
File, 31, 32, 132
File copying, database, 189
File creation, database, 178, 188
File, functional, 165, 166
File, indexed, 63
File, inverted, 67
File processing, 70–82
File, sequential order, 63, 64
File, serial, 78
File updating, 75–81, 127
File updating, database, 190
Financial accounting systems, 14
Financial modelling, 48
Financial systems, 14
Finding a record, database, 84, 193, 194
First generation computers, 5
Flowcharting, 106
Flowcharts, 107–112
Forms display, 84, 85
Forward chaining, 207
Fourth generation language (4GL), 89, 175
Full index, 65
Functional decomposition, 99
Functional files, 165, 166
Functional systems, 11, 12
Fuzzy logic, 206

Gateway, 215
General information, 21, 22
General nature of business systems, 11

Hardware, 42–44, 51, 53, 123, 124, 129, 130
Heuristic process, 207
Hierarchical database, 168, 169
Home-based electronic office, 7, 8

INDEX 249

Homeostasis, 29

IBM token ring, 216
Icons (ikons), 90
Image processing, 224
Indexed files, 64
Index sequential file, 64
Indexing, database, 183, 184, 193
Inference engine, 201
Inferencing, 202
Information, 21–26, 46
Information centre, 226
Information flows, *see* Data flow diagram
Information processing, 32–36, 63, 84–91
Information provider, *see* Public database
Information storage, 32
Information systems, 28
Information systems, computerised, 29
Information systems development, 93–115
Information systems, structure, 30–32
Information technology, 3–10
Information technology, advantages, 8, 9
Input, 138, 139, 146, 147
Input devices, 123, 129
Input documents, 132
Insertion, new records, 81
Instructions, 46
Integrated accounting packages, 232, 237
Integrated systems, 12–14
Interactive program, 90
Interactive video, 224
Interactive viewdata, *see* Public database
Internal memory, 42, 43
Inventory control, main menu, 147
Inventory control, report menu, 149
Inventory control system, 145–150
Inverted files, 67
Invoice, 122, 123

KBS, *see* Knowledge based system
Knowledge based system (KBS), 200–212
Knowledge engineers, 200

LAN, *see* local area network
Laser scanner, 245
Local area network (LAN), 3, 214, 215
Logical data, 172
Logical entity, 172

Maintenance, product file, 143
Management accounting systems, 14
Management by exception, 28, 29
Marketing system, 15

Mechanical accounting machine, 4
Megabyte, 43
Menu-driven application, 137–150
Menu selection, 86, 87
Merge sorting, 70
Methods, selecting a computer, 53, 54
Microcomputer, application, 127, 128
Modelling, 112
  financial, 48
Modem, 124
Monitor, 8
Monitoring devices, 30
Mouse, 90
MS-DOS, 45
Multi-tasking, 128
Multi-user systems, 128
Multiple Virtual Storage/System Product (MVS/SP), 45
MVS/SP, *see* Multiple Virtual Storage/System Product

Natural language processing, 87, 88
Network, 126, 214–219
Network database, 169, 170
Next pointer, 169
Nominal ledger, 14
Non-financial systems, 15

Office support systems, 226
On-line processing, 126, 127, 130, 131
Once only costs, 56
Operating costs, 51, 56
Operating system, 44, 45, 225
Order processing, 48, 131–133, 137–150, 209–212, 239–244
Order processing menu, 139
Order reporting menu, 141
Organisation, functions, 15, 16
Output, 34, 35, 132, 133, 140–142
Output devices, 123, 124, 130
Owner, 169

PABX, (Private automatic branch exchange), 7
Packet switched stream (PSS), 166
Parallel running, 56
Password, 8
Payroll data, 35, 36
Personnel, effect of information technology, 6, 7
Personnel records, database, 187–199
Personnel system, 15
Picking list, 140
Point-of-sale (POS) terminals, 244–246
Pointers, 90
POS terminals, *see* Point-of-sale terminals
Primary data, 30
Private automatic branch exchange, *see* PABX
Probability, 206

Processing, on-line, 126, 127, 130, 131
Processing operations, 32–36, 138–140, 146–148
Processing runs, 121, 122
Processing, serial, 63, 64
Processing techniques, 119–124, 126–133
Product data, 140
Product file, 147, 148
Product maintenance, 143, 148
Production system, 15
Program, 46
Program generator, 226
Profit and loss, spreadsheet, 158, 160, 161
Project planning, 48
Proposals, 55
Prototyping, 112–115
PSS, *see* Packet switched stream
Public database, 166
Purchasing system, 15

Query language, 175

RAM (Random access memory), 42, 43
Random access memory, *see* RAM
Random enquiries, 127
Random order file, 63
Read-only memory, *see* ROM
Real-time system, 129
Reasoning, 202
Record, 31
  insertion of new, 81
Relational database, 166–168
Reorder report, 149, 150
Report generator, 175
Role of computer, 46–48
ROM (Read only memory), 43
Relational structure, *see* Relational database
Retail terminal, 245
Ring network, 215, 216
Rules, 203, 204

Sales analysis, 141, 142
Sales, costs and profit, spreadsheet, 161–163
Sales ledger updating, 77, 78
Satellite transmission, 224
Schemas, 170
Screen displays, 84–86
Secondary data, 30
Self-indexing, 65
Sensor, 29
Sequential order file, 63, 64
Serial files, 78
Serial processing, 63, 64
Set, 169

Signal boosters, 216
Simulation, 48
Software, 51, 53
Sorting, 33, 70–75
Spreadsheets, 6, 155–164
Staffing, 51
Star network, 216, 217
Stock control, 15, 48, 145–150
Stock management, *see* Stock control
Stock transaction menu, 147
Stock transactions, 147
Storage, 32
Store and forward network, 219
Structured analysis and design, 93–103
Structured English, 104–106
Sub-schema, 170–172
System flowchart, 99, 107–112
  construction, 110, 111
  maintenance, 143, 144
Systems analysis, 95, 96
Systems Network Architecture Protocols, 216

Technological change, 6
Tenders and contracts, 54, 55
Telephone line, 8
Terminals, 8
Terms of reference, 95, 96
Transaction entry menu, 138, 139
Transaction history diagram, 96

Uncertainty, 204–206
Unit costs, spreadsheet, 157, 158
UNIX, 45
Updating, 34, 75–81, 122

VADS, *see* Value-added data services
Validating, 33
Value-added network, 219
Value-added data services (VADS), 224
Viewdata, 5
Virtual machine environment (VME/K), 45
Virtual machine/system product (VM/SP), 45
VME/K, *see* Virtual machine environment
VM/SP, *see* Virtual machine/system product
Volume of transactions, 52

Wages computations, 35, 36
What-if?, 48
Wide-area network, 3, 219
Windows, 91
Workstations, 5